GRACE WILLIAMS

GRACE WILLIAMS

Malcolm Boyd

UNIVERSITY OF WALES PRESS
ON BEHALF OF THE WELSH ARTS COUNCIL
1980

British Library Cataloguing in Publication Data

A catalogue record for this book is available from the British Library.

CORRIGENDA

p.10, line 26: for '1919', read '1917'.

p.20, line 15: for 'ex.10', read 'ex.9(*b*)': line 17 for '*proffwyd*', read '*broffwyd*'.

p.22, line 27: for 'Si lwli 'mabi', read 'Si hei lwli 'mabi'.

p.90, line 18 (The Burning Babe): date should read '1959'.

Printed in England by Bookcraft, Midsomer Norton, Avon

CONTENTS

PREFACE

This study, like others in the present series, is intended as a general introduction to the music of one important Welsh composer. In it I have adopted a mainly chronological approach and tried to place Grace Williams's music in the context of her life and career, but I have not attempted a full or detailed biography. This must be left to someone who enjoyed close personal contact with the composer, and who has access to all the archival material. There is room, too, for more than one view of the music, and it is gratifying to be able to report that Grace Williams's surviving scores have already attracted the attention of several students and scholars from England and Wales.

I am deeply indebted to the Executors of the Britten Estate, Aldeburgh, and to Vivien Cutting, Dorothy Gow, David Harries, Elizabeth Maconchy, and the late Gerald Cockshott for lending me letters and allowing me to quote from them. For permission to quote from published scores I am grateful to the Oxford University Press and the University of Wales Press. The Welsh Music Archive and its archivist, Ann Wyn Jones, kindly placed scores, tapes, and other material at my disposal, and I received valuable help from the staff of the BBC Libraries in Cardiff and London, the National Library of Wales, Aberystwyth, and the Parry Room of the Royal College of Music, London. I am especially grateful to Grace Williams's sister, Marian Glyn Evans, for allowing me access to the composer's manuscripts in Barry and for replying to innumerable inquiries with patience and enthusiasm. Among others who helped with information of various kinds I must mention Eiluned Davies, Ann Griffiths, J. Douglas Milbank, Enid Parry, Janet Price and Mansel Thomas.

Ruth Thackeray read the typescript and made many valuable suggestions, David Wyn Jones generously assisted in correcting proofs, and my wife participated actively in the book at all stages of its preparation.

M.B.
Cardiff, 1979

I CHILDHOOD AND STUDENT YEARS : 1906—1931

*I've grown to believe that it's against
nature for a woman to have talent for
anything except what's set down in the
last chapter of the Book of Proverbs*[1]

In some of the arts, notably literature, the creative role of women has been accepted in this country for a century and more, but the woman composer remains something of a rarity—something even of a phenomenon. The reasons for this are bound up with the whole history of women in musical society, a history which in all its fascinating detail lies outside the scope of this book. Even as executants women became involved in art music comparatively late. The attitude of the medieval and Renaissance Church, in whose devotions women were regarded as creatures barely to be seen and never to be heard, meant that their natural musical endowment, the high-pitched singing voice, was hardly available to the greatest composers until the 17th century. The rise of opera and its related genres, oratorio and the secular cantata, rendered women singers, if not indispensable, at least highly desirable (the Church's continued opposition led meanwhile to the rise of the castrato as an unnatural substitute) and by 1700 the prima donna was in the ascendant. Singers such as Francesca Cuzzoni, Faustina Bordoni, and Annamaria Strada were among the highest paid members of the musical profession in the early 18th century. As instrumentalists, on the other hand, women played an almost entirely domestic role before the 19th century, and the instruments they played were those which were harmonically self-sufficient or which could serve to accompany their own singing: the harpsichord, lute, guitar, and harp. Instruments used primarily in orchestral and ensemble music, and therefore entailing a measure of social intercourse, were left to the men.[2] Clara Schumann, wife of the composer, was perhaps the first woman to make a career as an instrumental virtuoso, and it was not until well into the 20th century that women began to be employed in symphony orchestras on an equal footing with men.

Because music-making at its most ambitious is essentially a social activity, it is hardly surprising that composition lagged behind painting and especially writing as an outlet for female creativity. Nor, in view of women's role as executants, is it surprising that the earliest women composers were primarily songwriters. Probably the first woman composer of any repute was the Venetian Barbara Strozzi (born *c*1625), the adopted daughter of the poet Giulio Strozzi. She was, significantly, well known as a singer and her extant works, most of them published at Venice between 1644 and 1664, are all vocal.

---

1. Grace Williams to Gerald Cockshott, 5 December 1948.

2. This is still the case in some countries with strongly patriarchal societies (e.g. Greece).

Even so, she remained for a long time an isolated figure, and few other women composers seem to have been active before the 19th century, when a number of songwriters (Fanny Mendelssohn, Maude Valérie White) and composers of piano music (including Clara Schumann) achieved considerable success. Cécile Chaminade (1857 — 1944) is also chiefl· remembered for her piano pieces, and she wrote a great many songs, but she was also perhaps the first to extend the range of the woman composer to include opera, ballet, and orchestral music. As a result of her example, and even more after the achievements of Ethel Smyth in England and Morfydd Owen in Wales, women composers of Grace Williams's generation in Britain no longer had to face the kind of prejudice that Dr. Johnson expressed towards women preachers in the 18th century. Grace Williams nevertheless felt the need to 'prove herself' in what was still predominantly a man's world, and when as a student at the Royal College of Music in London she found herself in the company of other young women with similar ambitions the awareness that they were 'banding together' was very strong.[3] The fact that no-one surveying the whole range and character of her music would be able to tell, without prior knowledge, that it was the work of a woman rather than a man is in part a measure of her success in the face of a long and inimical tradition, but her consciousness of that tradition coloured her whole outlook as a composer and touched her career in a number of important ways.

Grace Mary Williams was born in the coastal town of Barry, Glamorganshire, on 19 February 1906.[4] Her father, William Matthew Williams, was a schoolteacher from Caernarvon. He had met her mother, Rose Emily Richards, also a teacher, in Llanelli and they were married in 1900. Shortly afterwards they went to live at Wenvoe Terrace in Barry, and it was there that Grace, their first child, was born. By the time their second child, Glyn, was born (in 1908) they had moved to 9 Old Village Road, where they remained for the rest of their lives; a second daughter, Marian, was added to the family in 1919. Both parents were keenly interested in music, particularly Grace's father, whose Romilly Boys' Choir earned a reputation extending far beyond their home town. Grace was often employed as piano accompanist at choir rehearsals, but it was chiefly at home that she received her early musical education, and in the most practical way possible. Her father was not interested in guiding his children through the narrow hoops of piano 'grade' exams, but he did possess a useful library of music scores of all kinds, and these Grace was encouraged to explore. In this way her musical taste developed, and the operatic excerpts, oratorios, and keyboard music (above all that of Bach, Beethoven, and Chopin) that she found in her father's library sharpened her discrimination and laid the foundations of many later enthusiasms. Domestic music-making also included piano trios, with Grace playing the violin, her brother Glyn the cello, and her father the piano. (Had her sister Marian been born a few years earlier the ensemble would no doubt have expanded to a piano quartet.) Awareness of the wider world of orchestral music came

3.   A. J. Heward Rees: 'Views and Revisions', *Welsh Music*, v/4 (1976 — 7), 7.

4.   This is the date recorded on her birth certificate, but the event occurred about midnight, and at least one of those present maintained that the clock was slow and that the birth actually took place on the 20th.

principally from gramophone records, of which Grace's father was an avid collector even in those early days, and from local concerts in Barry and nearby Cardiff.

A scholarship from the junior school took Grace Williams to the Barry County School for Girls in 1917. She did well there, excelling in English, French, mathematics, and of course music. French was a particular enthusiasm, and she continued to take a keen interest in French literature all her life. She was later to pay many visits to France, on one occasion staying for several weeks *au pair* with a family in Le Lavandou, on the Côte d'Azur between Toulon and St. Tropez. A schoolfriend, Olga Price, has recalled how Grace

> enjoyed school and entered into every part of its life wholeheartedly, whether it was the annual Shakespearian play . . . or dancing, or the school orchestra, in which she played the violin.[5]

Another schoolgirl enthusiasm which was to remain with her into adult life was swimming; her diaries, up to 1959 at least, rarely fail to record the dates (and temperatures) of her first and last bathes each year.

There was at first no full-time music mistress at the Barry County School — a quite normal state of affairs at the time — and Grace was coached in music for what was then the School Certificate (now GCE 'O' level) by the school's geography teacher. But for her more advanced musical training it was thought necessary to engage a full-time music specialist, and Miss Rhyda Jones (later Mrs Basil-Williams) was appointed. Although still quite young (she had just graduated from University College, Aberystwyth, where she had studied under Walford Davies), Miss Jones proved to be a well-equipped and inspiring teacher. Under her guidance Grace successfully completed her Higher School Certificate (the equivalent of the later GCE 'A' level) and gained a scholarship which enabled her to study at University College, Cardiff. During her last years at school she began also to show her talent for composition, and she would take her young teacher, week by week, small pieces (mainly songs and dances) that she had written on the beach at Cold Knap in Barry, close to the sea that was so often to inspire her maturer compositions.

The university music department at Cardiff was, when Grace Williams entered it in 1923, quite typical of such departments in the kind of training it offered, and in particular in the emphasis placed upon technique (harmony and counterpoint) as an academic discipline. The professor was David Evans, composer of a number of large-scale choral works but known throughout Wales chiefly as a choral conductor and adjudicator. Grace Williams found the social life at University stimulating — she was an attractive girl, much in demand at student dances and other social functions — but the BMus course itself she later described as 'deadly', and as far as original composition was concerned she felt herself to be a prisoner. Opportunities existed for practical music-making, but composition, if it could be called that, went little further that the invention of academic fugues and minuets to prescribed formulae.

The biggest opportunity for would-be composers in the department came with the 'exercise' that each student was expected to complete as part of the final examination. For

---

5. 'Grace Williams: a Symposium (Part 2)', *Welsh Music*, v/7 (1977 — 8), 58.

this Grace Williams chose to make a setting for soloists, chorus, and string orchestra of Shelley's poem *To Night*. It is, as one might expect, an immature piece of work with few really good ideas, but it is interesting in showing an early orientation towards Wagnerian harmony and textures (see ex.35, page 77) and towards structures which seek to unite elements of suite and symphony. The speed and character of its four movements give the work an overall symphonic shape, with the quickest movement (not really a scherzo) placed second and the slowest third; but no attempt is made to unify the movements thematically or in any other way, except by a rudimentary tonal scheme which keeps too much of the music tied to B (minor or major) and G sharp minor. The looseness of the structure is emphasized by the diversity of the scoring: the first and last movements are for five-part chorus, the second for solo mezzo-soprano, and the third for four soloists (S, A, T, B); the string orchestra plays in each movement except the third, which is unaccompanied. *To Night* is one of Grace Williams's earliest extant works. It owes its preservation to the fact that the only surviving score was kept in the University archives and was therefore out of the composer's reach.

If Professor David Evans was able to do little himself to develop and train Grace Williams's compositional talent, he did at least recognize it. No doubt recalling the example of Morfydd Owen, who had trod a similar path some 15 years earlier, he recommended her to apply for admission to one of the London colleges on completion of her BMus degree at Cardiff. Morfydd Owen had pursued her studies at the Royal Academy of Music; Grace Williams applied to the Royal College, and in 1926 she became a pupil there of the composer Ralph Vaughan Williams.

Vaughan Williams had been teaching at the Royal College since 1919, in which year he had accepted the invitation of the director, Sir Hugh Allen, to come up to London one day a week 'and be yourself'. Being himself meant that he made his experience available to students 'as counsellor and fellow-artist rather than judicial authority'.[6] Only students who, like Grace Williams, already had some inkling of what composition was about could have profited from a mentor who would criticize a piece of work with the remark: 'I know there's something wrong, but I can't put my finger on it'.[7] Nevertheless the advice and encouragement of 'Uncle Ralph', as he was affectionately known to his students, was valued highly and was eagerly sought by many even after their formal training had come to an end. The direct influence of Vaughan Williams's own music on his younger British contemporaries was, of course, enormous and not in every way beneficial; Grace Williams succumbed to it less than did many others, as we shall see — far less, for example, than another of Vaughan Williams's Welsh pupils, Arwel Hughes.

As is often the case at this particular stage in a young person's education, the time spent in the company of fellow students at the Royal College of Music was at least as important to Grace Williams's development as the formal teaching she received. It happened that her contemporaries included several of the same age and sex as herself, and

6.   A. E. F. Dickinson: *Vaughan Williams* (London, 1963), 66.

7.   A. J. Heward Rees: 'Views and Revisions', *Welsh Music*, v/4 (1976 – 7), 8.

together they made a formidable circle of young women composers, or would-be composers: Dorothy Gow, Imogen Holst, Elizabeth Maconchy, and Elisabeth Lutyens. (The last named was not a pupil of Vaughan Williams and therefore did not come into Grace Williams's immediate circle until later on, when both composers were active in promoting contemporary music through the Macnaghten Concerts in London.) Grace Williams was on particularly close terms with Elizabeth Maconchy, and their friendship continued and deepened during the next 50 years, both through personal contact and in a long and (for the biographer of either composer) important exchange of letters. They carried on the habit instigated by Vaughan Williams of hearing and criticizing each other's work; scores were exchanged and discussed to their mutual advantage in a collaboration which recalls a similar one which Gustav Holst and Vaughan Williams engaged in for many years.

In 1928 Grace Williams achieved her earliest success as a composer when her *Fantasy Quintet* for piano and strings was awarded second prize in the Cobbett Chamber Music Competition at the Royal College (the first prize went to Imogen Holst). In common with most of her early pieces the quintet has not survived, but we do have a handful of songs to give some idea of the kind of music she was writing at the time. It is impossible now to say which is the very earliest of them, since she did not adopt the practice of dating her compositions until much later, but among them is a setting for soprano and small orchestra of Psalms 137 and 126. This was written in 1927, during or just after her first year at the RCM, and revised in the 1930s; it is the first work of any importance that the composer did not withdraw — an opus 1 in all but name. Not surprisingly, the style is derivative of the kind of music the leading English composers were writing at the time. Vaughan Williams's influence is detectable above all in the suave modality and the smooth string counterpoint of the second psalm. Despite their modal (and chromatic) inflexions, the two songs employ a securely tonal idiom, the first being in C major and the second in E flat minor. But it is also possible to discern certain stylistic features that were to assume considerable importance in Grace Williams's later works: the rhythmic suppleness of the music, particularly in the first psalm with its 7/8 metre; the alternation of two triads with roots or basses separated by a tone or a semitone; the importance in both melody and harmony of the sharpened ('Lydian') 4th and of the ambivalence between major and minor 3rd; and the nice balance of lyricism and declamatory expression in the vocal line. Some of these features are observable in the opening of the first psalm, 'By the waters of Babylon' (ex.1, overleaf; bars 1—2 are here omitted).[8] Perhaps the least personal (and in the light of the later works the most surprising) aspect of these songs is their scoring, which is for flute, clarinet, trumpet, harp (or piano), and strings. The maturer composer would surely have preferred the oboe to the clarinet (especially for texts expressing the lamentation of the Jews in captivity) and she would certainly have written differently for the trumpet, which here serves mainly to provide a bass for the wind instruments — a role that might have been more effectively taken by a bassoon.

---

8. This music was used again for the final sequence in the incidental music for *Esther* (1970).

Ex. 1

[harp omitted]

Vaughan Williams's influence is still discernible in another song, *Service of All the Dead* (D. H. Lawrence), probably dating from two years later (1929). Indeed, one might have supposed it to have been suggested by the 'Dirge for Two Veterans' in *Dona nobis pacem*, were it not that the Vaughan Williams piece was not composed until 1936. Once again the idiom is not strongly personal, and the song's main interest now lies in its being the earliest extant example of the processional manner that was to inform many of the composer's later orchestral pieces. Other songs that can be definitely assigned to the RCM years include *Slumber Song* (Siegfried Sassoon) and *They closed her eyes* (John Masefield). It is worth remarking that in both of these, as in most of the other songs written before about 1950, Grace Williams used an instrumental ensemble rather than a simple piano accompaniment.

Among the awards available to composition students at the RCM was the Octavia Travelling Scholarship, designed to assist deserving students to complete their training abroad. In the summer of 1930 Grace Williams was awarded £50 under the terms of this scholarship (once again coming second to Imogen Holst, who was offered twice this amount) and she elected to study with the Austrian composer and scholar, Egon Wellesz, in Vienna. Wellesz (1885–1974) may seem a strange choice in view of the kind of music that Grace Williams was to write later, and one wonders what guided her to make it. It is unlikely to have been admiration for Wellesz's own music, which was hardly known at that time in this country — and, indeed, has remained little known ever since, despite the fact that Wellesz later settled in England and taught at Oxford University from 1938. Nor can it have been the fact that he had been a pupil of Arnold Schoenberg and had published a book on that composer, since neither then nor at any later stage did Grace Williams confess to a particular sympathy for Schoenberg's music or for Schoenbergian techniques. What may possibly have attracted her to the idea of studying with Wellesz (apart from his reputation as a teacher) was the Austro-German late Romantic tradition, which lived on in Vienna, and in this she and Wellesz must have found a great deal in

14

common. She had for some time been a devotee of Wagner's music (much to the exasperation of some of her student colleagues) and her own music was soon to reflect a close acquaintance with Strauss's as well. Her love of Mahler's music, which was also to prove a powerful influence, came later, however, possibly as a result of her friendship with Benjamin Britten; in 1930–31 she actually disliked it, and said as much to Wellesz.

Where Vaughan Williams had been vague and encouraging, Wellesz was precise and analytical, and Grace Williams found his teaching of immense value. As she later commented, he had a way of saying: 'It begins to get weak at this point, so you will scrap from here and re-write'.[9] Like all wise composition teachers he made no attempt to impose a particular idiom on his students or to direct them along favoured stylistic paths, and one looks in vain for any sudden metamorphosis in the works of Grace Williams that have survived from the early 1930s. The paucity of extant scores and the difficulty of dating them precisely make it impossible to form a true estimate of Wellesz's impact on his pupil. The only work that is known for certain to have been written in Vienna is the Violin Sonata, dated November 1930. It is not a piece that many would consider worthy of revival now, and although it was revised in 1938 all but the second movement failed to satisfy the composer's maturer scrutiny. Dating from about the same time, and possibly also composed in Vienna, is the Sextet for piano, oboe, trumpet, and string trio (the choice of wind instruments is significant in view of Grace Williams's later predilection for them). Both works are derivative of those composers whose music most attracted her at the time, combining (not altogether successfully) the neo-modalism of Vaughan Williams, the proliferating textures of Wagner and the later Romantics, and (in the first movements particularly) the aggressive dissonances and restless rhythms of Bartók. The sextet is the more indicative of the path her music was to take later in the 1930s, especially in the Romanticism of such passages as ex.2 (overleaf) from the first movement. It is, however, the finale of the work, with its modernistic penchant for perfect and augmented 4ths, that sets the style for the music she wrote in the years immediately following her return from Vienna.

Two chamber works of this period seem to represent a conscious attempt to come to grips with that flank of the avant garde represented by such composers as Hindemith in Germany, Poulenc in France, Walton in England, and (at that time) Bartók in Hungary. While belonging chronologically to the next chapter in this survey, they can be regarded in a sense as student works since they employ a style and reflect an aesthetic which the composer was soon to reject. The Sonatina for flute and piano, an undated work performed at the Macnaghten Concerts in the 1930s, illustrates these new trends admirably and affords some striking points of contrast with the Violin Sonata and the Sextet. Vestiges of Classical sonata form remain, but there are now no lengthy passages of literal restatement and what recapitulation there is is allusive and aphoristic. Flowing modal counterpoint is replaced by spare, transparent textures in which the solo line is only lightly accompanied or, for quite long stretches, not accompanied at all. Tonality

9.   A. J. Heward Rees: 'Views and Revisions', *Welsh Music*, v/4 (1976–7), 8.

Ex. 2

remains fundamental to the structure, but the warm, neo-modal harmonies of the earlier works give way to athletic 4ths and piquant 2nds, with here and there a hint of bitonality (ex.3). It is difficult to escape the impression that in this work and in the Suite for nine

Ex. 3

instruments, which dates from a few years later, Grace Williams was attempting to sound 'modern' for the sake of sounding 'modern' — a natural and even laudable thing for a young composer to do.

It is significant that this exploratory period in Grace Williams's development should result primarily in abstract chamber works, ideal for testing compositional techniques

16

whether on paper or in performance. The few such works that date from the years after 1934 are all short and insubstantial, and chamber music finds almost no place at all among her mature compositions, a fact which she often excused by saying that she had no talent for it. It would be nearer the truth to say that her mature style could find appropriate expression only in orchestral and vocal music, and for this no apology was needed. Wagner, Strauss, and Mahler are not called to account for having written little or no mature chamber music, and Grace Williams's failure to do so was for much the same reasons as theirs. Present ignorance of the early chamber works leaves a gap in our total appreciation of her art, and a performance to-day of the Flute Sonatina or the Suite for nine instruments would raise many eyebrows. But Grace Williams was to find her way forward in music of quite a different kind.

II LONDON AND LINCOLNSHIRE : 1932—1945

In 1931 Grace Williams's brief period of study came to an end and she left Vienna. At the age of 25, with her formal education behind her, the time had come to look for permanent employment—something to be found more easily in London than in Wales, as her compatriot Mansel Thomas also discovered at about the same time. During her years at the RCM she had already done some part-time schoolteaching, and so she was not entirely without experience when, on 1 January 1932, she began her duties as a visiting lecturer at Southlands Training College, Wimbledon Park Side, with a salary of £81. This was increased in September to £108, and in the same month she became also music mistress at the Camden School for Girls in north London. Neither post was full-time, but together they brought her enough to live on and a little over which enabled her to attend concerts and opera in London and to visit the Continent with friends during the summer vacations.

Grace Williams's interest in children and young people was instinctive and genuine, and she made an unusually good teacher. Her pupils responded warmly to the seriousness and enthusiasm she showed towards them and towards her subject, while she, in return, was able to benefit as a composer from the practical experience that schoolteaching brought. Opera had always been a passion with her, and her diaries of this period record frequent visits to the theatre to see *Tristan und Isolde*, the *Ring*, *Der Rosenkavalier*, *Tosca*, and other masterpieces of the lyric stage. At Camden High School she had the opportunity, not to say the obligation, to produce operas, and under her guidance the girls performed the usual Gilbert and Sullivan repertory as well as such works as *Hansel and Gretel* and *The Bartered Bride* in versions skilfully adapted by her to the resources of the school. Such practical stage experience, even at a relatively modest level, proved to be of great value when she came to write her own opera some 20 years later.

Demanding and exhausting though her teaching duties must have been, they still left time at weekends and in the evenings for original composition, and the vacations, spent mostly in Barry, allowed more extended periods of creative work. The music that Grace Williams composed at this time was mainly orchestral, beginning with the overture *Hen Walia*. This is in fact the earliest orchestral piece for which a score still exists, and it was the first of her works to achieve frequent performances; it was broadcast a number of times in the 1930s but fell out of sight (and hearing) during World War II. The composer was to evoke the spirit of ancient Wales in a more original way in the works she wrote some 25 years later, but it is not difficult to understand why *Hen Walia* should have been popular, for it strings together a number of attractive folktunes and folklike tunes (with the well-known lullaby *Huna blentyn* as a broad centrepiece) and places them in a stirring, energetic setting which seems to suggest a mixture of Vaughan Williams and Walton. The orchestration may not show the originality of Grace Williams's later scores, but it is remarkably skilful, imaginative, and assured; one must presume the destruction of a number of prentice works for orchestra.

Stylistically *Hen Walia* belongs to Grace Williams's earliest period; it is perhaps the most successful of the works reflecting the influence of her teacher, Vaughan Williams, and his English contemporaries. A better structured and more forward-looking work, however, is the *Elegy* for string orchestra, composed in 1936. At that time it no doubt exemplified just one of the various stylistic paths that Grace Williams's music might have followed in the mid-1930s, but its opening bars display a number of features that were to assume increasing importance in the music of the next 20 years or so (ex.4). Perhaps the

Ex. 4

most radical of these is its shadowy tonality; there is no key signature, and the veiled suggestion of C sharp major that comes with the first chord does not receive triadic confirmation until the very end. An interesting technical feature of these bars, and of many other passages in the piece, is that they are constructed from a mode of alternating tones and semitones, and this contributes immeasurably to the feeling of tonal instability in this and many later compositions.[1] The elegiac mood of ex.4 is beautifully sustained and developed during the rest of the piece, and the music's intensity of feeling, especially at the climax (five bars after letter D, coinciding with an enharmonic restatement of the first chord, *ff*), suggests that it may have been written in response to some deeply felt personal experience; there is no dedication, however, to indicate what this might have been. The *Elegy* was given a number of performances during the years immediately preceding World War II and was revised in 1940. It was later withdrawn, but it would do the composer's reputation no disservice were it to be heard again now.

1.   The use of this mode probably derives from the composer's interest in Bartók's music, but it has been widely used by other Welsh composers, including William Mathias, Alun Hoddinott, Daniel Jones, and David Harries. It is also one of Messiaen's 'modes of limited transposition'. Its relevance to Grace Williams's music is summarized elsewhere (see pages 79–80).

The last and most ambitious of Grace Williams's pre-war orchestral works has the title *Four Illustrations for the Legend of Rhiannon* and is based upon incidents from the *Mabinogion*, that great medieval treasure-house of ancient Welsh legend, history, and folklore. Each of its four movements illustrates part of the first branch of the *mabinogi*, the story of Pwyll, Lord of Dyved. The first, a stormy, impassioned movement entitled 'The Conflict', tells of the rivalry between Pwyll and Gwawl, son of Clud, for the love of Rhiannon, the beautiful daughter of Heveydd the Old: 'And thereupon Pwyll's household came down upon the palace and seized all the host that had come with Gwawl and cast them into prison'. The second movement, 'The Nuptial Feast', is descriptive of the marriage feast for Pwyll and Rhiannon: 'And they went to the tables and sat down. And they ate and feasted, and spent the night in mirth.' The third movement deals with the penance Rhiannon was forced to make for having supposedly killed her son, Pryderi; it takes the form of a sombre chorale prelude on the Welsh hymn tune *Hen Ddarbi*, later used by the composer in the slow movement of her Violin Concerto (see pages 31 — 2 and ex.10).   The final movement, telling of how Teirnon Twrvliant slew the monster that had snatched Pryderi away and of Rhiannon's reunion with her son, also uses a traditional Welsh air, *Cainc Dafydd proffwyd*, as its main theme. It strongly recalls a theme in the first movement of Sibelius's Second Symphony.

Despite the evident intention of giving it an overall symphonic shape (the second movement has the character of a scherzo and the third functions as a slow movement),[2] the work remains disjointed and episodic. Only the first two movements are at all convincingly shaped, and even then the quality of the music rarely rises above that of a good film score. On a technical level, too, the Rhiannon *Illustrations* represent a withdrawal from the radical position occupied by the *Elegy*. Their musical language is more conservative, harking back to the idiom of the early works, particularly in the last two movements (later discarded), in which the introduction of traditional material entails the use of key signatures once more. Grace Williams was to tackle again the problem of symphonic narration on a large scale in the *Symphonic Impressions* of 1943, but it was one she was never to solve with complete success.

During the 1930s Grace Williams wrote a number of solo songs with orchestra which were of the utmost importance in placing the voice at the centre of her musical thinking and establishing stylistic links (by no means usual among British composers of the time) with the Strauss — Mahler tradition. *The Song of Mary*, a setting of the Magnificat (St. Luke, i, 46 — 55) for solo soprano and orchestra (oboe, trumpets, trombones, harp and strings), is the last and probably the finest of these. It was composed in 1939, revised in 1940 and again in 1945, and is in many ways similar in style to the *Elegy* for string orchestra. The solo line, freely structured and often ecstatic in expression, soars above a shifting chromatic texture (once again there is no key signature) to which a persistent accompaniment figure, established by the strings in the opening bars, brings a convincing structural unity. The harmonies are warmer than those of the *Elegy*, making expressive

---

2.   The original title was 'Symphonic Legend: Rhiannon'.

use of the chromatic appoggiaturas and non-functional 'dominant' 7ths that were to remain a feature of the composer's style at least until the Violin Concerto. Towards the end the music lingers on what might be called the 'Elegy' chord' (see ex.4, above), before resolving (as the *Elegy*) did onto a serene C sharp major triad.

The key of C sharp, whether major or minor, seems to have held a particular fascination for Grace Williams at this stage, just as G minor had in some early works (Violin Sonata, Sextet) and as other tonalities were to do later on. C sharp is found again as the basic (or at least the concluding) tonality of *Gogonedawg Arglwydd*, another work dating from 1939. Except for her BMus exercise, *Gogonedawg Arglwydd* is the earliest choral work of any substance in Grace Williams's extant oeuvre. It was also, it seems, her first setting of a Welsh text, the words being from the 12th-century Black Book of Carmarthen, and if only for this reason it was something of a disappointment to her that the work was never performed in Wales during her lifetime. It would be pleasant to be able to report the discovery of a neglected masterpiece. *Gogonedawg Arglwydd* is hardly that, and its duration (just over five minutes) makes it a difficult work to programme; it is also somewhat retrospective in style, the triadic switch from B flat minor to D major near the beginning recalling the opening of Vaughan Williams's *Sea Symphony*. But Grace Williams's handling of words was never less than competent, and *Gogonedawg Arglwydd* constitutes an effective setting of a text similar to that she was to use with more distinction in the *Benedicite* (1964). It would make a bright opening to a choral and orchestral concert, or a suitable anthem for a festive church occasion.

Among Grace Williams's close friends during the 1930s was the composer Benjamin Britten, who lived near her in south-west London after her return from Vienna. Britten valued highly her judgment in musical matters; he would play to her his latest compositions and take very seriously any criticisms she might make. The two composers spent a great deal of time in each other's company at concerts and the opera, and occasionally at the cinema; in April 1936 Britten suggested that she should accompany him on a visit to the Continent. They were together at Covent Garden when Britten saw Wagner's *Tristan und Isolde* for the first time, an experience which left him 'speechless and starry-eyed'.[3] Although he was Grace Williams's junior by nearly eight years, Britten was at this time already much better known as a composer than she was, and his friendship was therefore a source of great encouragement to her. It was partly through his recommendation that she was invited to write music for films, and he was influential, too, in getting his publisher, Boosey and Hawkes, to accept the *Six Welsh Oxen Songs*—'by far the best arrangements of any folk-songs I know'.[4]

The war of 1939—45 brought to an end Grace Williams's personal friendship with Britten, although the two continued to correspond afterwards from time to time. In 1939 Britten left for the United States, and at the beginning of that September Grace Williams

---

3.   Grace Williams to Robert and Lilli Hille, 8 December 1976.

4.   Benjamin Britten to Grace Williams, ?25 September 1934.

resigned her post at Southlands Training College and left for Uppingham, Rutland, where the Camden High School was installed at the outbreak of war. Subsequently the school moved across the county border to Lincolnshire, first to Grantham and then to Stamford, where Grace Williams found lodgings at 15 Ryhall Road.

Like Britten, Grace Williams was a pacifist and she would have been opposed to war at any time; but the conflict with Hitler's Germany could hardly have come at a worse time for her own composing career. The immediately preceding years had seen a growing number of performances, particularly of the *Elegy* and *Hen Walia* but also of the ballet music *Theseus and Ariadne* and smaller works such as the *Cavatina* for string quartet (now lost). Performances did not altogether cease during the war years, but they inevitably became less frequent, while new works had to wait longer before being heard (neither *The Song of Mary* nor *Gogonedawg Arglwydd* received its first performance until 1945). The trials and upsets of the war did not, however, completely interrupt the work of composition, and these years saw the creation of four important orchestral pieces, two of which were soon to bring Grace Williams's music before a much wider audience than she had addressed hitherto.

The first of these was the *Fantasia on Welsh Nursery Tunes*, completed in 1940 and first performed, in a broadcast by the BBC Northern Orchestra conducted by Eric Fogg, on 29 October the following year. Soon it was being heard all over the country and before long it was recorded for the Decca company by the London Symphony Orchestra under Mansel Thomas. Even to-day it remains the work by which the composer is best known. Lasting about ten minutes, the Fantasia quotes eight traditional nursery songs in the following order:

1.	bar 1: Jim Cro	5.	letter H: Gee, geffyl bach
2.	letter B: Deryn y Bwn	6.	letter J: Cysga di fy mhlentyn tlws
3.	letter D: Migildi, Magildi	7.	letter N: Yr eneth ffein ddu
4.	letter F: Si lwli 'mabi	8.	letter Q: Cadi ha!

Little attempt is made to integrate or combine the eight melodies, but *Jim Cro* returns at the end to round off the piece. Such works as Vaughan Williams's Norfolk Rhapsodies and his various Fantasias on traditional tunes probably served as models and, like her teacher, Grace Williams connects the traditional melodies with original but stylistically appropriate material which accommodates numerous changes of key, tempo, and mood.

Despite its popularity and the special affection the composer always reserved for it, the Fantasia cannot be numbered among her most successful works. For Welsh listeners there will always be the delight of sharing in the culture evoked by the traditional melodies; but it is impossible to ignore the fact that the harmonizations are often heavy and conventional, and the structure loose. Nor does the much praised orchestration have the zest of, say, Alun Hoddinott's *Welsh Dances* or William Mathias's *Celtic Dances*, although it is proficient and practical enough, and (like many of Vaughan Williams's orchestral scores) adaptable to various resources. The Fantasia did much to make Grace Williams's name known, and for this reason it occupies an important position in her output; but it revealed little of her potential as a serious composer, and there is no reason to regret that she never felt moved to capitalize on its success with another similar work.

Grace Williams now turned her attention for the first time towards abstract symphonic works, beginning with the Sinfonia Concertante for piano and orchestra, completed in 1941 and first performed in January 1943. An early pencil draft, still extant, shows that it was originally conceived as a piano concerto, but none of its three movements places the soloist in a dominating role and there is no cadenza. To this extent the final title more accurately reflects the nature of the composition, but the piano part, expertly laid out for the instrument, is nonetheless in the grand Romantic manner stemming from Liszt and Tchaikovsky, and it requires a powerful virtuoso technique. The music itself is also full-bloodedly Romantic in style, with passages (especially in the slow movement) that recall the concertos of Russian composers such as Rakhmaninov, Medtner, and Skryabin, as well as (less comfortably) some of the wartime film scores written in the shadow of such masters. If the work fails in the end, it is because it lacks the thematic character and inspiration to reinvigorate what to modern ears must seem an outworn tradition. A future age may find its derivative gestures less crippling, and may be able to respond with unself-conscious abandon to such passages as the impassioned climax of the central Lento (ex.5) — a movement linked in mood (and in key) to the *Elegy* of 1936.

Ex. 5

The Sinfonia Concertante was written at Grantham, but as far as the character of the music is concerned it might have been composed anywhere between Glasgow and

Gorlovka. In other works written during the years of exile in London and Lincolnshire Grace Williams remained more conscious of her Welsh background, and many of them embody some aspect of Welsh history, landscape, or culture. A good example of this is the First Symphony, completed in 1943. Its full title, on one of the surviving manuscripts at least, is *Symphony no. 1 in the form of Symphonic Impressions of the Glendower Scene in 'Henry IV Part 1'*; the composer usually referred to it simply as *Symphonic Impressions*. The first three of its four movements are musical portrayals of the character Owen Glendower in Act III scene 1 of Shakespeare's play, each one illustrating a different facet of his character. The first, showing Glendower as a mighty warrior, is prefaced by Shakespeare's lines:

> At my nativity
> The front of heaven was full of fiery shapes
> Of burning cressets; and at my birth
> The frame and huge foundation of the earth
> Shak'd like a coward.

The music is mainly restless and turbulent, with brass fanfares suggesting the warlike Glendower and the battles of Welsh history. The movement contains some of the most dissonant and aggressive music that Grace Wlliams had so far composed, and its impact is reinforced by the resources of a large, Romantically proportioned orchestra. Gradually the sounds of battle recede and a calm, folklike theme, with typically Welsh 'Lombard' rhythms, is heard on a muted trumpet in a key (E major) often associated in music of this period with moments of repose (ex. 6). One might suppose this to be the second subject of

Ex. 6

some vast Mahlerian sonata structure, especially when it is repeated with string counter-points over a prolonged pedal E; but there is only the briefest return of the 'battle' music and, after a *misterioso* passage for strings and woodwind (letter T), the movement ends with an abrupt D minor chord.

The second movement depicts Glendower the dreamer, and it takes its cue from his translation of words spoken in Welsh by his daughter to her husband, Edmund Mortimer:

She bids you
Upon the wanton rushes lay you down
And rest your gentle head upon her lap
And she will sing the song that pleaseth you
And on your eyelids crown the god of sleep,
Charming your blood with pleasing heaviness . . .

The languorous quality of the richly chromatic outer sections (the movement is in ternary form, A — B — A) results largely from the gentle oscillation of major and minor 3rds, a stylistic fingerprint already present in earlier works and one that was to become even more prominent in the later music. The central episode is somewhat retrospective in its diatonically modal style, and this suggests (as does the state of the manuscript itself) that the movement was written some time before the other three.

The third movement, entitled 'Scherzo barbaro e segreto', is an impression of Glendower the magician and is prefaced by the passage from Shakespeare beginning 'I can call spirits from the vasty deep'. Glendower's braggart claims and Hotspur's taunting dismissals are suggested in high-powered, agitated music with little or no respite for lyricism, although the 'trio' section (not so called in the score) is more delicately scored. Like several of Vaughan Williams's symphonies the work ends with an epilogue. Here the composer puts aside Shakespeare's characterization and attempts, in her own words, 'a retrospective impression of Owain Glendwr, great figure of Welsh history'. Beginning in the style of a heroic funeral march, with muffled drums measuring a steady tread, the music gradually assumes a more elegiac tone, and indeed the '*Elegy* chord' (see ex.4, above) is present more than once; moreover the work ends in Grace Williams's elegiac key of C sharp, but this time with a minor 3rd.

The scoring of the *Symphonic Impressions* was completed on 7 July 1943, but there was at that time no prospect of a performance; the days when the composer would be asked to write major works to commission, with performance guaranteed, were still in the future. In November 1947 Sir Adrian Boult tried it through with the BBC Symphony Orchestra, but it was not until 30 March 1950 that it was publicly performed — by the BBC Welsh Orchestra conducted by Mansel Thomas. Two further broadcasts followed in 1952, one from Scotland and the other from Wales, after which it seems to have dropped from the repertory. The composer soon afterwards withdrew all but the Scherzo, which was performed for a time as a separate piece. As with all her major works, the symphony contains many things that one would dearly like to hear again, but it is not difficult to understand the composer's dissatisfaction with it as a whole. Except for the Scherzo, the large-scale structures tend to be slack, and there are long passages, particularly in the first two movements, where the music seems to drift or to be pushed aimlessly along. Possibly the composer was aware of this, since a number of cuts, amounting in all to 30 bars of music, were made in the first, second, and last movements after the work had gone into rehearsal (or perhaps after one of its early performances). But the excisions do not save the work, and neither as a character study nor as symphonic music can it be compared with Elgar's *Falstaff*.

Although flawed, the *Symphonic Impressions* merit attention for their consistently interesting orchestration and because they demonstrate better than any previous work the composer's handling of tonality in this period. As it happens, the work begins and ends in the same key (or its enharmonic equivalent), but this observation does not apply to each individual movement, as the following summary shows (keys refer to the tonality in which each movement begins and ends):

1. Allegro con fuoco: D flat major → D minor
2. Andante liricamente: B major → B major
3. Scherzo barbaro e segreto: E flat major → E flat major
4. Epilogue, Andante solenne: B flat minor → C sharp minor

It would be misleading to equate Grace Williams's methods here with the so-called 'progressive tonality' of Nielsen. They have more in common with Mahler's approach to tonality in such works as the Seventh and Ninth Symphonies, and it is interesting that 'Neapolitan' relationships loom large in Grace Williams's key schemes, as they do in Mahler's. The sequence of keys in the *Symphonic Impressions* seems to be directed neither by structure nor by expressive considerations (except those that might have existed in the mind of the composer), and this might be said with almost equal truth about the internal tonal organization of each movement. In short, its tonal waywardness weakens the structure, and it is surely no coincidence that the works of Grace Williams's artistic maturity (those written from about 1955 onwards) show a much stronger feeling for tonal balance and unity.

With the scoring of the *Symphonic Impressions* completed, Grace Williams returned to Camden High School at the end of the summer vacation in 1943, but not this time to Lincolnshire. Unaware of the flying bombs that Hitler was to hurl at London during the ensuing months, the school had returned to the capital, and Grace Williams found accommodation at 30 Willow Road, Hampstead, where she was to remain until her return to Wales. Vacations spent with her parents in Barry continued to provide opportunity for physical relaxation and artistic sustenance, and her next major work was directly inspired by the Glamorganshire coastline near her parents' home. This was the *Sea Sketches* for string orchestra, completed in 1944 and dedicated 'to my parents who had the good sense to set up home on the coast of Glamorgan'.

The *Sea Sketches* had to wait for performance until 31 March 1947, but the work soon established itself as one of Grace Williams's most successful pieces, rivalling (but not exceeding) the *Fantasia on Welsh Nursery Tunes* in popularity. It is a much better work than the *Fantasia*, and unquestionably the finest thing she had written up to that time. In 1951 it became her first substantial work to achieve publication — by the Oxford University Press, who subsequently undertook publication of a number of other works. The five pieces that make up the suite are all scored with a player's understanding of string music, and they paint vivid pictures of the sea in various moods. The gusts blowing in 'High Wind' and the rolling of the tide in 'Breakers' are powerfully suggested; 'Channel Sirens' is a particularly striking evocation, with its desolate, repetitious fog-horn sounding on violas and cellos and its misty chords on the upper strings (ex.7). Despite the dedication,

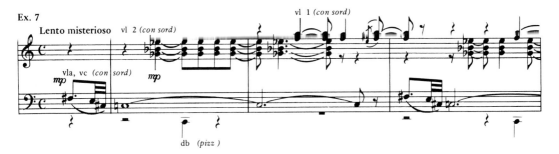

Ex. 7

Lento misterioso

there is little in the music to suggest that the seascapes are specifically Welsh, and in the last piece, 'Calm Sea in Summer' (in the serene key of E major), it is possible to imagine the composer lazily dreaming of the Viennese days when the sounds of Mahler and Strauss lapped against her musical consciousness. Indeed there are passages where the effect of richly proliferating textures and sumptuous chromatic appoggiaturas approaches the autumnal world of Strauss's *Four Last Songs* (a work still in the future, of course) (ex.8).

Ex. 8

(Andante tranquillo)

III RETURN TO WALES : 1945—1954

I shall henceforth live in Barry
which will be a much healthier and
easier life—and there'll be the sea[1]

The next ten years were the least productive in Grace Williams's entire career as far as new concert works were concerned. The difficulties and deprivations of the war years, the efforts she had made on behalf of the Camden High School, and the need to use her leisure time in composing and copying music had left her exhausted and in poor health. The years immediately following the war brought the most serious physical, emotional, and artistic crisis she was ever to live through. As early as October 1944 her diaries begin to record visits to doctors in Harley Street and Wimpole Street, and by the end of the year she had become seriously ill and was forced to spend eleven days in hospital. For a time it looked as if she would have to give up composing altogether, and in fact on her discharge from hospital she did resolve very seriously to do so. She was encouraged in this by a Polish friend, Zenon (Zen) Sliwinski, to whom she had become deeply attached, but probably her physical condition and the doubts she always felt about the value of her work had something to do with it as well. In August 1945 she wrote to Dr. Gerald Cockshott, another Vaughan Williams pupil whom she had first met two years earlier:

> I have now succeeded in putting composing out of my mind for good and all. I rescored the Song of Mary and that was the final touch. It just wasn't possible to carry on any longer with two dynamic jobs. It's a grand feeling to be free of it, and not having it tugging at my conscience any more—and lovely having plenty of time for reading—and thinking about so many other things. I'm really looking out for a full time non-teaching job—something quiet for a change, though I shan't like it too much at first as I've been so used to going all out on a job. The difference to me since I stopped composing is amazing—people at home who saw me at Easter almost twice the size can't make it out.[2]

About two months later she wrote:

> I don't want to stay in London—I just long to get home and live in comfort by the sea and have a well-paid full-time job which isn't teaching . . . I like the children and I've always liked teaching them—but I'm sick to death of the succession of school functions, dingy school buildings and—you know all the rest . . .[3]

1.   Grace Williams to Gerald Cockshott, n.d. (postmark 10 December 1946).

2.   Grace Williams to Gerald Cockshott, n.d. (postmark 10 August 1945).

3.   Grace Williams to Gerald Cockshott, n.d. (postmark 19 October 1945).

Applications for a lectureship at University College, Cardiff, and for an assistant inspectorship with the London County Council came to nothing, but an opportunity to exchange schoolteaching for something else presented itself in 1946 when a vacancy occurred in the Schools Broadcasting department of the BBC. On May 24 Grace Williams was interviewed for the post, which she was offered and which she accepted. The fortnight from June 19 to July 3 was spent in University College Hospital, and when term ended on July 26 she said goodbye for the last time to Camden High School. On September 2 she took up her new appointment with the BBC but, as it turned out, this was to last for only a few months. Her duties included writing radio scripts, arranging music, and visiting schools, all of which she found interesting and rewarding; but her illness persisted and soon she was being advised by her doctors to return to Barry where she could be properly cared for. By the middle of December she had resigned her post and on 21 February 1947 she vacated her rooms at Willow Road. Four days later she arrived with her belongings at her parents' home in Barry, where she was to live for the rest of her life.

If the decision to return to Wales was to a considerable extent imposed upon her, it was nevertheless a risky one to make. Without independent means a freelance composer could hardly exist except by taking the occasional arranging, teaching, and lecturing that was offered from time to time, and such opportunities were likely to be fewer in South Wales than in London, where she had made valuable contacts. The situation in South Wales was nevertheless much brighter than when she had left University College, Cardiff, in 1926. During the 20 years since then a separate Welsh Broadcasting Region had been set up by the BBC in Cardiff, with its own music department and orchestra (reconstituted and strengthened in 1946); the Welsh National Opera had been founded; the Welsh Office of the Arts Council had been set up; and soon there would be a new College of Music and Drama and annual music festivals in Swansea and Cardiff. In the years to come Grace Williams was to receive support from all these organizations, but London contacts were not broken off. On her return to Barry a good deal of creative energy was channelled into writing scripts for school broadcasts and incidental music for the BBC and for film companies in London. Apart from such 'jobs', as she referred to them, she continued for some time to regard herself as retired from composing.

The first radio play for which Grace Williams supplied incidental music was probably *Hannibal* by Robert Gittings, broadcast by the BBC in June 1947. During the next two years she collaborated on three plays with the author Henry Treece, the most important from a musical point of view being *Rataplan*, a fantasy based on an anonymous 16th-century French poem. The score was completed in the unusually short time of eight weeks, so that the programme could be entered for the Italia Prize in 1949. The music, lasting some forty minutes, is continuous and cost the composer a great deal of effort; but it seems never to have been broadcast. In subsequent years Grace Williams wrote music for radio and television productions of plays by Saunders Lewis and she also collaborated on at least four films between 1948 and about 1956. Of these the most important was probably the prize-winning *David* (1951) of Paul Dicksen, made for the Welsh Committee of the Festival of Britain. Writing incidental music was a lucrative occupation, but it had the disadvantage, especially as far as broadcasting was concerned, that the fate of the music was bound up with the (usually) short life of the production. From the music for Henry Treece's *The Dark Island* (1948) Grace Williams was able to compile a four-movement suite for string orchestra, and the 'Mountain Sequence' from the film *Blue Scar* (1948) also achieved several independent performances. But for the most part the incidental music of these years, which represents a sizable part of her total output, is now beyond recall.

Also unlikely ever to be heard again are the numerous folksong and carol arrangements that Grace Williams made for the BBC schools programme 'Rhythm and Melody' between 1946 and 1954. These are all straightforward arrangements, skilfully done but without any claim to originality. The only ambitious work to result from her involvement with children's programmes was *The Merry Minstrel*, a version of the Grimm brothers' fairy tale *Der wunderliche Spielmann* for narrator and orchestra. In this very young persons' guide to the orchestra the minstrel of the title demonstrates his skill on every orchestral instrument (not just the violin, as in the Grimms's original), in the process out-witting a wolf, a fox, and a hare. Comparison with Prokofiev's *Peter and the Wolf* (1936) is inevitable, and it must be admitted that Grace Williams's work suffers by the comparison. *Peter and the Wolf* had the advantage of a stronger narrative, a young hero that children can identify with, and more memorable tunes. But *The Merry Minstrel* has its own virtues: it can be enjoyed by younger children, and its coverage of the orchestral instruments is more systematic and comprehensive than Prokofiev's.

The urge towards resuming original composition (as distinct from 'jobs') seems to have begun in 1948 when, 'through sheer frustration and bad weather, and an excess of family',[4] Grace Williams began work on a Piano Concerto, using up some of the sketches she had made for *Blue Scar* and incorporating part of the *Dark Island* music. At least one movement of the concerto was finished in rough score, but in the end the project proved abortive, possibly because the effort of filling long symphonic structures proved too much after years of producing short snippets for film or play sequences. By the end of 1948 the composer was again in the doldrums, as her letters to Gerald Cockshott indicate,[5] and meanwhile she was finding it increasingly difficult to make ends meet on the income she derived from her 'jobs'. By the summer of 1949 she was even contemplating a return to London.

> I'll go to London next month, and it will probably be in search of another full-time job (which will *really* mean the end of composing this time). I've managed to keep going until now — but prospects aren't good and I can't live on air.[6]

4. Grace Williams to Gerald Cockshott, n.d. (postmark 7 September 1948).

5. See, for example, the extract quoted at the head of Chapter 1 of this book.

6. Grace Williams to Gerald Cockshott, n.d. (postmark 2 August 1949).

But hopes of permanent employment in the capital came to nothing:

> I had a lovely time in London but had no luck over jobs—except for some editing and arranging of school choruses for O.U.P. which I can do whenever I like—it won't bring in money for ages—but may prove a worth while investment. From now until Christmas I'm having my last fling at composing . . . I've started on a Violin Concerto . . . [7]

The Violin Concerto, the only really important orchestral work from the decade at present under review, was completed in February 1950 and first performed the following month with its dedicatee, Granville Jones, as soloist. It embodies at its most fluent that strain of ardent Romantic lyricism which had been present in Grace Williams's music ever since the *Elegy* of 1936. This quality invests the concerto with an emotional appeal unparalleled in any of her works of comparable size, even if most listeners will probably feel the lack of textural and rhythmic contrast to be a weakness in the long run. The first movement is a beautifully shaped piece, characteristically marked *liricamente,* with broad, sweeping lines for the soloist supported by warm harmonies and luxuriant orchestral textures (see ex.39); its seamless structure reaches a climax of Straussian intensity (four bars after letter N) which is followed by a short virtuoso cadenza and a brief recollection of the opening. It is a fine movement, but should it not, like the leisurely paced first movements of Walton's concertos, be followed by a scintillating scherzo, or at the very least by a relaxed Allegretto?

Grace Williams's second movement is an Andante sostenuto, roughly the same in pulse-rate and duration as the first movement. It takes the form of a meditation on the Welsh hymntune *Hen Ddarbi,* which had already been used for the third of the *Four Illustrations for the Legend of Rhiannon.* In the concerto only the first phrase of the tune is used, and it is so set around with soloistic decoration and orchestral commentary that one could easily fail to identify it. It would require close comparison of the two movements to show how Grace Williams's style changed and her compositional skill matured during the eleven years that separate them; but ex.9 (overleaf) shows typical treatments of the *Hen Ddarbi* tune, and will give some idea of the sort of change that has taken place. It will be noted that the modal D of the melody has been sharpened in the concerto version, removing what would be an exotic, recalcitrant feature in this context. The finale, tied to the second movement by a single thread of cor anglais tone (F sharp), widens at last the expressive spectrum of the work. It is a sonata-form Allegro, somewhat reminiscent of Prokofiev in style and in the panache with which the suggestion of a march is held at bay by lyrical episodes and energetic passage-work. The coda brings a second cadenza, longer and more brilliant than that in the first movement, before the music winds down in a delicately scored *diminuendo.* A final unexpected (and perhaps unwelcome) *ff* chord reinforces a tonic (C) which has been unusually prominent for a work of this period.

The Violin Concerto is no masterpiece, but it represents the best that Grace Williams achieved during the first half of her creative life and a revival of it would be welcome. It is

---

7. Grace Williams to Gerald Cockshott, n.d. (postmark 30 October 1949).

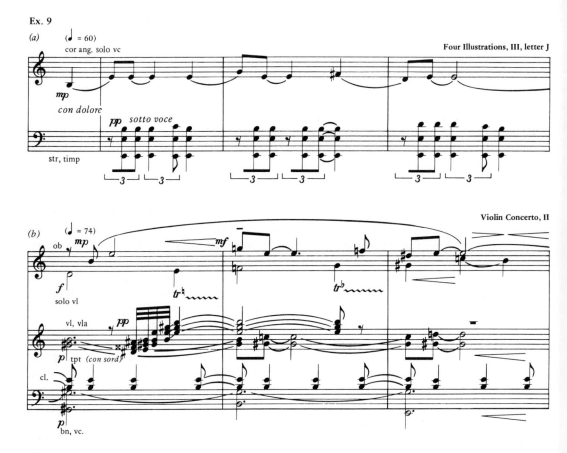

one of a number of works which the composer would certainly have revised if she had lived a few more years. However, she showed no inclination at the time to follow it with another large-scale orchestral work, and in any case BBC and film 'jobs' continued to take up most of the time available for composition. This was diminished in January 1950 when she took up a part-time teaching post at the recently established College of Music and Drama, then housed in Cardiff Castle; and in 1954 she was forced through financial need to add to her non-creative commitments the drudgery of copying other composer's music. The extent to which the lack of uninterrupted periods of composition affected her work and gave rise to feelings of frustration is conveyed in an undated letter to Elizabeth Maconchy:

> I'd struck a barren patch — had got so used to doing 'jobs' that when I found I was free to write what I liked I felt lost without the props and ideas the 'jobs' had provided. It was awful — struggling and scrapping and switching from one thing to another. Then last week I thought I'd found what I wanted — something (perhaps a serenade) for two harps and orchestra — and I got started in real earnest and the old feeling of being full

of it returned—Then of course the inevitable happened—I got caught up in the nightmares of pedalling . . . Anyway I've now got interrupted . . . The only thing I'm proud of is that I've done loads of revision of old scores—a great weight off my mind. And I've written lots of scripts (the great standby if I dry up as a composer).

Nothing seems to have survived of the 'serenade', and a great many other works were consigned to the waste-paper basket at various times. An entry in her diary for 10 May 1951 records one of the composer's occasional purges:

DAY OF DESTRUCTION Examined all my music manuscripts and destroyed nearly all which I considered not worth performing.

This entry, written in red ink, illustrates the intense self-criticism (if that is what it was) that led the composer to destroy works which many others would have been pleased to call their own. But possibly it reveals also a measure of dissatisfaction with her *modus componendi* as a whole. Certainly as far as orchestral music was concerned there was soon to be a move away from the Romantic textures and harmonies of the *Symphonic Impressions*, the *Sea Sketches*, and the Violin Concerto towards a more economical, more personal, and at the same time more distinctively Welsh mode of expression.

This was not to become apparent until 1955, however. The immediately preceding years produced only two light and relatively unimportant orchestral works, the Hornpipe *Keel and Anchor* (1953) and *Seven Scenes for Young Listeners* (1954), both of which received several radio performances. More important is the choral suite *The Dancers* (1951), a setting for soprano, women's chorus, harp, and string orchestra of five poems by various writers, with dancing as a common theme. Except for her student work, *To Night*, and the brief *Gogonedawg Arglwydd* (1939), this is the first of Grace Williams's choral works to survive, and yet nowhere does it betray any lack of experience in choral writing or in word setting. In tracing the course of her development from the Violin Concerto to the Second Symphony its easier-going rhythmic and harmonic style might appear to constitute an irrelevant or even a retrograde stage, but some concessions to the nature of the texts and the possibilities of the medium were obviously necessary. In *The Dancers* diatonicism keeps a fairly tight rein on the harmonic texture, and key signatures are employed throughout. This does not signify, however, a return to Classical principles of tonal unity, either within a movement or over the work as a whole. The first song begins in A major, the last ends in E major, and none of the five songs begins and ends in the same key. A *laisser faire* attitude towards tonal progression prevails, as before, with extensive use of pedals for stability and coherence.

The first song introduces the solo soprano in a charmingly fresh setting of some Cypriot verses. In style (and in key) it recalls the 'Barcarole' of the *Dark Island* suite and anticipates in a similar way the first of the Hopkins settings (1958). The sharpened 4th is a typical and consistent feature of the song (and of the other two works just mentioned); also characteristic of the composer are the alternation of A major and B major chords over a tonic pedal and the triadic outlines of the vocal melody (ex. 10). The second song is a racy choral setting of Belloc's well-known *Tarantella* ('Do you remember an inn, Miranda?'), which Grace Williams had set as a solo song in 1930, and soloist and chorus

Ex. 10

come together for the first time in Chatterton's *Roundelay*. This desolate lament is perhaps the most impressive number in the cycle. The soprano repeats eight times, each time at a different pitch, a refrain whose intense, grief-laden melancholy is heightened by the contrast it makes with the repetitive, impersonal chanting of the chorus (ex.11). Also

Ex. 11

using a refrain, but this time for structural rather than expressive purposes, is the fourth song, May Sarton's *Lose the pain in the snow*, and the suite ends with a spirited setting of Kathleen Raine's *To the wild hills* which to some extent recalls the first of the *Sea Sketches* and more strongly foreshadows the 1975 setting of Beddoes's *To Sea! To Sea!*

Joan Sutherland, later to achieve international fame on the operatic stage, was the first soloist in *The Dancers* on 18 November 1954, with the Penarth Ladies Choir conducted by Arwel Hughes. It is to be regretted that the composer never made a version of the work for mixed choir; such an arrangement would certainly have increased its popularity, and might even have enhanced its effectiveness.

IV YEARS OF MATURITY : 1955—1971

It would be an exaggeration to suggest that Grace Williams, in her development and progress as a composer, turned the kind of stylistic corners that Stravinsky did, for example, but it is possible to recognize in the music she wrote after about 1954 a new sense of direction and an individuality not often apparent in the large-scale works she had written before that date. The First Symphony, the Sinfonia Concertante, and the Violin Concerto had employed late Romantic forms and idioms with considerable technical assurance, but not always with sufficient melodic vitality to give them new life, while the popularity of the *Fantasia on Welsh Nursery Tunes* was not altogether the result of any particular musical distinction. Only in the *Sea Sketches* and *The Dancers*, among the large-scale pieces, had artistic ambition been consistently matched by creative imagination, and these, significantly, were both suites rather than symphonic works. If she were judged only on the music she had written by 1955, when she was almost 50 years old, Grace Williams would seem to-day a very minor composer indeed; any claim to regard her as one of Wales's finest composers must rest principally on the music she wrote during the remaining twenty years of her life.

The true nature of this quite sudden maturing as a composer was no doubt buried deep in her psychological make-up, but it manifested itself above all in a new self-confidence and a stronger sense of identity. Her earlier works had frequently incorporated traditional Welsh melodies (the *Fantasia* being by no means the only example) and had been inspired by Welsh history (*Symphonic Impressions*), landscape (*Sea Sketches*), or contemporary life (film music for *David*), but the composer had rarely attempted to throw off the late Romantic, essentially Teutonic cloak that had been her inheritance. To some extent the stylistic dichotomy that this implies persists in the later works, most of which could easily be given a 'nationalistic' or 'cosmopolitan' label. But the Welshness of, for example, *Penillion*, *Ballads for Orchestra*, or *Castell Caernarfon* is no longer dependent on the outward trappings of text, folksong, and so on; nor is it in conflict with a late Romantic idiom. On the contrary, it is able to fertilize it into producing something new. Some of the features by which this quality of Welshness may be recognized will be identified as this volume proceeds, but it is worth remarking here that not a single original work written after 1954 uses a Welsh folktune.

As well as a new maturity one notices a renewed fecundity during this period; major works follow each other in a steady succession. This is partly a concomitant of the new self-confidence reflected in the music, but it was also dependent, as always, on outward circumstances. With live and broadcast performances becoming increasingly frequent Grace Williams was able to lay aside some of the tasks that had until now stood in the way of her original work. We hear nothing during these years of any professional copying activities (other than those connected with her own music) and in 1953 or 1954 she gave up her part-time teaching post at the College of Music and Drama. Her thrice-yearly assignment of folksong and carol arrangements for the BBC, which had occupied untold hours since 1946, also seems to have come to an end at this time. To a considerable extent she remained financially dependent on 'jobs', and the demise in 1964 of the BBC Children's Hour, for which she had continued to write scripts, meant a sudden and substantial loss of income. But an increasing supply of commissions helped to support the modest (some would say Spartan) life-style to which she had become accustomed.

To a composer commissions are not merely a source of income; they provide a measure of the public and critical acceptance his work commands — an indication that his music is actually wanted. Recalling her first commission, received just before the war from the BBC in Wales, Grace Williams said:

> You know it was a marvellous sensation, simply being asked to write something; someone wanting your music. Once I got going on it the music absolutely haunted me. I went about London, and even when travelling on the underground the music was still there in my head. Such was the elation of having a commission, the ideas flowed freely.[1]

It was this kind of recognition that brought Grace Williams the deepest satisfaction. Any kind of adulation that she felt to be insincere embarrassed her, and official honours were usually declined.

The main events affecting Grace Williams's personal life during the period at present under review were the deaths of both her parents, whose home she had shared since her return to Wales. On 5 June 1957 her father was presented with the freedom of Barry in recognition of his long and distinguished service as conductor of the Romilly Boys' Choir — a proud moment for the whole family, and not least for Grace, whose early musical training had been closely bound up with that choir. Ten days later her father was taken ill, and on the morning of June 20 he died. Grace's mother survived him for five years, living to celebrate her 90th birthday before she too died on 4 June 1962, 'looking very beautiful and serene', as Grace lovingly recorded in her diary. For the rest, the story of these busy years is mainly one of steady hard work: composing, writing out scores and parts, supervising rehearsals, and attending performances and recordings. Somehow time was still found for public work (she was an active member of the Composers' Guild), for teaching and coaching, and for listening to the music of her contemporaries.

It is convenient to divide the music Grace Williams wrote during these sixteen years into three categories, each one productive of a large-scale major work. First there is the orchestral music, including the Second Symphony; secondly the solo songs, along with which may be considered her only opera, *The Parlour*; and finally the choral works, among which towers the *Missa Cambrensis*. It is in this order that the works will be surveyed in the present chapter; the chronological arrangement that has so far prevailed is therefore relaxed.

---

1. A. J. Heward Rees: 'Views and Revisions', *Welsh Music*, v/4 (1976 – 7), 13.

Orchestral Music

The work that more than any other signals the beginning of a new phase in Grace Williams's artistic development is *Penillion*, written for the National Youth Orchestra of Wales in 1955. The title refers to the ancient Welsh practice of *penillion* singing, in which a traditional tune on the harp is repeated as an accompaniment to newly improvised counterpoints by the singer. William Leathart described it in 1825 as follows:

> Pennillion chaunting . . . consists in singing stanzas, either attached or detached, of various lengths and metres, to any tune which the harper may play; for it is irregular, and in fact not allowable, for any particular one to be chosen. Two, three, or four bars having been played, the singer takes it up, and this is done according as the Pennill, or stanza, may suit — he must end precisely with the strain, he therefore commences in any part he may please. To the stranger it has the appearance of beginning in the middle of a line or verse, but which is not the case. Different tunes require a different number of verses to complete it; sometimes only one, sometimes four or six.[2]

In its pure state, which has been much debased in modern times, the improvisatory element in *penillion* singing was hedged round with all kinds of metrical and other 'rules'. For the purposes of a modern orchestral piece Grace Williams did not attempt to observe the strictest traditions of *penillion*, but in its combination of a rigid stanzaic structure and quasi-improvisatory melodic lines her composition retains two of the strongest features of the tradition. The orchestration includes an important part for the harp (Wales's national instrument could hardly have been omitted from such a work) but it would, of course, be impossible for the harp to play its traditional role here and the recurrent melodies are entrusted to other instruments, often a solo trumpet. Traditional melodies are not used, as they are in true *penillion* (almost certainly they would have been if the piece had been written ten years earlier), but the music as a whole has a distinctly Welsh flavour which is rarely to be found in Grace Williams's earlier works, even in those that use actual folksongs. This has a great deal to do with the way the musical rhythms echo the stresses of the Welsh language. For example, the accent on the penultimate syllable of polysyllabic words, a feature of the language, is paralleled in the music by phrases which end with an accented short note followed by an unaccented long one (see exx. 12 – 14, below).

These are by no means the only features of traditional *penillion* to be found in Grace Williams's piece. Others include a simple harmonic framework and the essentially narrative style adopted by the singer, whose 'counterpoints' were always declamatory rather than melodic or lyrical. Still another is the practice referred to in William Leathart's definition of delaying the singer's entry until after the start of the harp melody. Some of these features may be illustrated from the first movement of *Penillion*, in which the basic 'harp' melody (the composer's own, it must be stressed) is played first by the trumpet, supported by strings and harp, with trombones mainly reinforcing the bass, and the woodwind linking each phrase of the melody (ex. 12). For the second 'stanza' the melody is

---

2. W. Leathart: *Welsh Pennillion* (London, 1825), 12–13, quoted in W. S. Gwynn Williams: *Welsh National Music and Dance* (London, n.d.), 83. For an example of *penillion* to the melody *Llwyn onn* see *ibid*, pp. 103–4.

Ex. 12

repeated an octave lower on first horn and cellos, with a counterpoint initiated by the second trumpet (ex.13; note how the new counterpoint begins after the start of the main

Ex. 13

melody — a feature which extends to each stanza and each movement). Next the melody passes from the cor anglais to the oboe and then to the clarinet and flute, with a fresh counterpoint (*liricamente*) which is shared first between the same instruments before passing to the first violins (ex.14; note this time the new pitch inflexions of the main melody). There are two further stanzas in which both the basic melody and its decora-

Ex. 14

tions are less sharply defined, although the stanzaic structure remains clearly perceptible.

Fundamental to the structure of this and similar movements (not only in *Penillion*) is the principle of variation, but the form cannot be labelled as 'theme and variations' in the generally accepted sense. Of all the older variation forms it has most in common with the strophic variations of early Baroque cantata and opera, with the important distinction that in *Penillion* it is the melody and not the bass that forms the recurring, stable element. That the structure is capable of serving a wide range of expression is demonstrated in the other three movements. The second is a kind of scherzo, introducing a decidedly dithyrambic, if not demoniacal (and not very Welsh!) element that is to be encountered more than once in subsequent works. It is followed by a slow movement in D minor, alternating 3/4 and 2/4 metres in a four-line stanza which is heard five times in all. A richly Romantic movement this, in which some of the most expressive and memorable phrases are heard in the interludes between each stanza, particularly at bars 56 − 8 and 90 − 92. The last movement, in which the relatively strict *penillion* structure is somewhat relaxed, is dance-like in character like the second, but this time with its high spirits firmly rooted in a native benevolence.

Although best described as a suite, in the number and character of its movements *Penillion* is given an overall shape which might be called symphonic. The principle of tonal unity is still denied to the work as a whole (the last movement being in A minor), but key signatures are present and each movement is securely anchored in a particular key. This is to a large extent imposed by the structure itself, but it becomes increasingly the ·norm in Grace Williams's music after *Penillion*. Also symphonic, but probably unintentional, is the transference of motifs from one movement to another, notably the following (ex.15):

Ex. 15

40

These are both melodic fingerprints to be found in other works as well, and the second (ex.15*b*) is also omnipresent in Vaughan Williams's music. The element of development in the way that one stanza succeeds another also verges on the symphonic, as Arnold Whittall has pointed out.[3]

The idea of adapting the ancient traditions of *penillion* to a modern orchestral piece was a simple but brilliantly original one, and something that could hardly be repeated. However, a work in many ways akin to *Penillion* is *Ballads for Orchestra*, written thirteen years later for the National Eisteddfod in Grace Williams's home town. Like *Penillion*, *Ballads* has four movements, each using a stanzaic structure. The music has little in common with 19th-century ballades such as those of Chopin and Brahms. On the other hand, the literary form of the ballad (and Grace Williams's spelling of the title suggests that this is what she had in mind) strongly appealed to the composer as a song writer, and the narrative element in the composition is even more prominent than in *Penillion*. The score affords no clue to what the *Ballads* narrate, but the composer said of the work:

> I want to write something that's a synthesis of medieval Welsh laments, proclamations, feasts, combats — broad tunes — with a lot of free contrapuntal commentary.[4]

Ballads is more declamatory in tone than *Penillion*, and more dramatic; both the harmony and the orchestration (done this time with fully professional players in mind) are sharper-edged, and its lyricism is less overtly vocal in style. The first movement nevertheless qualifies its Allegro moderato tempo with the direction *alla canzone*, and its long-phrased melodic lines, imprinted with the so-called 'Scotch snap' or 'Lombard' rhythms characteristic of Grace Williams's declamatory manner, sound a note of impassioned lament underlined with minatory insistence by relentlessly pounding quavers in the bass (recalling perhaps the opening of Brahms's First Symphony, in the same key). The second movement is a solemn march, perhaps a funeral march, Mahlerian both in its repetition of a banal but insidiously memorable tune (compare the slow movement of Mahler's First Symphony) and in the orchestral textures that clothe it, particularly at the opening (ex.16). The third Ballad breathes that deep calm, tinged with an acrid wistfulness, that is characteristic of some of Grace Williams's most personal utterances. Intrusions by roulading clarinets and ominous brass, first separately and later (briefly) together, ruffle the calm without permanently disturbing it. Possibly they presage the unbridled vehemence of the final Allegro furioso, made the more truculent by its jagged 5/8 and 7/8 metres. Disheartened perhaps by the indifferent performances this far-from-easy suite received during her lifetime, the composer expressed reservations about its value as a whole. Possibly it lacks some of the freshness of *Penillion*, but it is nevertheless a not unworthy successor to it.

Except for the relatively unimportant but wholly representative *Castell Caernarfon*, composed in 1969 for the investiture of Prince Charles as Prince of Wales, *Ballads* was

---

3.   A. Whittall: 'Grace Williams 1906—1977', *Soundings*, no.7 (1978), 20.

4.   Grace Williams to Vivien Cutting, 28—9 November 1967.

Ex. 16

Grace Williams's last work for orchestra. Her best achievements as an orchestral composer during the years that separate *Penillion* and *Ballads* are shown in two works with solo instrument and the Second Symphony. The Second Symphony was first performed at the 1957 Swansea Festival. According to the composer's diaries the piano score was completed on 9 May 1956, the full pencil score on August 31, and the complete fair copy on November 2. Earlier in the same year she had celebrated her fiftieth birthday, and one wonders whether, as she worked on the symphony, she ever recalled a letter written on 22 January 1949 to her friend, Gerald Cockshott:

> Ten years ago I thought that no one could ever possibly want to hear music written by a woman in her forties. Well, the two Elizabeths [Elizabeth Maconchy and Elisabeth Lutyens] have proved me wrong. But I still feel the same way about women of 50 + . There does seem something revolting — and perhaps a bit pathetic — in the thought of a symphony by a woman of 50. Don't you agree?

No-one who has heard Grace Williams's Second Symphony could possibly agree.

In many ways the symphony has more in common with the music Grace Williams was writing before 1955 than with *Penillion* and the orchestral works that followed. There is, for example, no overall tonal centre, and although each movement begins and ends in recognizably the same 'key' there are no key signatures either. There is also little sign of the 'Welsh' features that have been identified above in *Penillion* and *Ballads*. There are four movements, as in the First Symphony, but this time there is no avowed program-matic intention behind the work. Allegro marciale is the tempo direction for the first movement, and yet the music conveys no very strong impression of a march, its trumpet calls, side-drum taps, and brusque string and wind octaves suggesting something more *marziale* than *marciale* (ex.17). These opening bars leave the listener guessing at a key,

Ex. 17

and he must go on guessing throughout the movement. It does become possible to postulate A flat as the tonal centre, but this is not buttressed by any hierarchy of subor-dinate and related pitches, much less by triadic harmony; only at the very end of the movement is A flat decisively established. The music's thematic structure, too, is resistant to the analytical norms applicable to first movements of late Romantic symphonies. A change of speed and metre (from 4/4 to 6/8) for the second main theme (bar 56) tends to loosen the structure, and would do even more if the transition from one tempo to another were less skilfully effected. It is just possible to recognize the outlines of a sonata structure, however, and this may be summarized as follows:

bars 1 – 35:	first subject (Allegro marciale, 4/4)
bars 35 – 56:	transition (*liricamente*, 4/4)
bars 56 – 76:	second subject (Poco meno mosso, 6/8)
bars 77 – 144:	development of first subject (Tempo I, 4/4)
bars 145 – 181:	development of second subject (Poco meno mosso, 6/8)
bars 181 – 252:	recapitulation and further development of first subject (Tempo I, 4/4)
bars 252 – 281:	coda, using material from transition and first subject (*a tempo*, 3/4 – 4/4)

In performance one is aware of a much tighter cohesion than this summary might imply, and this results mainly from the ubiquitous anapaestic rhythms derived from the opening trumpet phrase (see ex.17) and the intervals of a 3rd that pervade the whole movement.

This movement reveals an uncompromising, even forbidding, aspect of Grace Williams's musical personality which had never been evident to such a degree in her earlier compositions; it is surely no accident that some passages seem to recall the more aggressive parts of Vaughan Williams's Sixth Symphony. Also unusual, perhaps unprecedented, is the predominance of linear textures. With the gentle pastoral oboe melody that opens the second movement (Andante sostenuto) we seem to be on more familiar ground, and yet the simple unchanging drone of the accompaniment (violins, gently touched in by the harp) is uncommonly austere. As the movement progresses the melody becomes clothed in warmer counterpoints, more in the composer's later style (although the second and third movements were in fact completed before the other two), but the music remains curiously withdrawn. The scherzo, by contrast, has a grim purposefulness which, by thematic cross-reference, is carried even into the more relaxed 'trio' sections.

For a four-movement symphony in the Romantic mould to close with a slow finale almost inevitably raises expectations of an elegiac or valedictory ending; one thinks of Tchaikovsky's Sixth Symphony or Mahler's Ninth. The last movement of Grace Williams's Second Symphony begins in a way which seems to promise fulfilment of such expectations. There is something elegiac and autumnal, something Mahlerian too, about the *tranquillo* opening, with its gently acerbic semitonal clashes and its thrusting chromatic lines (ex.18). The material is developed at some length, incorporating (from

Ex. 18

bar 27) a new quintuplet semiquaver figure of a kind frequently present in Grace Williams's later music; but at length the trumpet calls from the opening of the first movement (see ex.17) are heard again, as if from some distant battlefield, and they increasingly impinge on the music as other material from the first movement is recalled. Finally the *marziale* elements completely dispel the elegiac ones, and the symphony ends on the same expressive plane as did the first movement.

But not in the same tonality. The absence of any powerful tonal drive, or even of a basic tonal centre, although by no means unprecedented in Grace Williams's music, is surprising in a work of such proportions. Still more surprising, and to many early listeners disconcerting, was the uncompromisingly aggressive tone of much of the music, especially in the first and third movements and the last part of the finale. But although it is unlikely ever to be numbered among the composer's most popular works, the symphony did reveal hitherto unsuspected dimensions to her artistic personality, and in the context of her music as a whole it can be seen to have played a cathartic role similar to that of the Fourth Symphony in Vaughan Williams's development. Without it her subsequent essays in suite and concerto (genres arguably more fitting for the natural expression of her ideas) would probably have been less satisfying.

Arnold Whittall was right to suggest that the Second Symphony was brought to completion 'against the grain'.[5] In February 1956 the composer wrote to Elizabeth Maconchy:

> Have at last got down to [my Second Symphony] — just finished the sketch of the scherzo, and started the slow movement. I have been in despair over it — thought I was past it and ought to give up the commission — then I did get going on this scherzo. It's rather ugly — and it never possessed me as I used to get possessed by what I was writing. I put in a lot of real plodding — it came spontaneously only in spurts — then a full stop for a while. Now I've finished the sketch I think it adds up quite logically and sounds alive even if it is a bit of an ugly duckling.[6]

The references to the music's 'ugliness' are interesting; Vaughan Williams used to talk in much the same way about his own Fourth Symphony. And signs of struggle are certainly present in the music, even after the revisions of 1975 which improved the continuity and cohesion of the finale.

After the Second Symphony there came a gap in Grace Williams's output of orchestral music until the *Processional* of 1962, a Llandaff Festival commission. This is a piece of about nine minutes duration in the composer's new declamatory style, suggestive (in her own words) of 'the solemnity and grandeur of ecclesiastical processions'. It was followed in 1963 by one of the finest of all her works, the Trumpet Concerto, written for and dedicated to Bram Gay, then principal trumpeter in the Hallé Orchestra. The composer's affection and special feeling for the trumpet had already been demonstrated in many orchestral works (including *Processional*) and it might have been predicted that she would eventually write a concerto for the instrument.[7] Her particular association with it may owe something to her experience of regimental bands during World War I:

> Barry was full of training camps and battalions marching through the streets with bands playing. If I remember rightly there was a fine regimental band which gave concerts in the park round the corner. When I grew older — and wiser — I became a pacifist; but the lure of cornets and bugles persisted, and perhaps paved the way for my entanglements with the orchestral trumpet.[8]

But another source of her interest in the trumpet may have been the orchestral scores of Mahler, who frequently brought the instrument into prominence as a soloist (for example at the opening of Symphony no.5) and wrote for it in a lyrical style.

5. A. Whittall: 'Grace Williams 1906 — 1977', *Soundings*, no.7 (1978), 20.

6. Grace Williams to Elizabeth Maconchy, 6 February 1956.

7. A *Movement* for trumpet and orchestra was composed in 1932. It was later withdrawn.

8. A. J. Heward Rees: 'Views and Revisions', *Welsh Music*, v/4 (1976 — 7), 15.

The Trumpet Conerto develops further the intensely Welsh declamatŏry style of *Penillion* and *Processional*, the opening bars of the first movement providing a glossary of some of the technical features that contribute to that style (ex.19; two introductory bars are here omitted). One of these is the 'Lombard' rhythm (accented semiquaver followed

Ex. 19

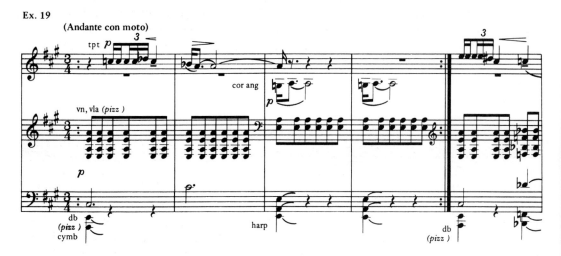

by unaccented dotted quaver) familiar from the music of Purcell and the pre-Classical period, but here serving expressive ends that link it with the verbal accents of the Welsh language; the triplets in the solo trumpet part are another distinctive rhythmic feature of the style. The ambivalence of major and minor 3rds (C sharp and C natural) is also characteristic, while the sharpening of the 4th and the flattening of the 2nd, 6th and 7th degrees of the scale (in the passage immediately following ex.19) serve to transform the A major suggested by the key signature into a kind of chromatically inflected Phrygian-cum-Lydian mode found extensively in the music of this period. The inclusion of the harp in the orchestra adds another touch of national colour. From this declamatory opening the music proceeds in a fairly orthodox but far from rigid sonata form, with a second subject suggesting martial fanfares in a key (B flat minor) which the first theme had obliquely hinted at. The two main themes are combined in a brief climactic restatement before the music veers away from A major to end calmly and expectantly in C, the tonality of the slow movement.

In trumpet concertos of the Baroque period the solo instrument was usually silent during the slow movements, partly because the brilliant technique that Baroque trumpeters cultivated would have been out of place there and also because the mechanism of the instrument (or rather the lack of it) made it difficult to sustain a line outside the fundamental key, usually C or D major. Haydn, writing for Anton Weidinger's keyed trumpet, was able to keep the soloist employed in the Andante of his concerto (1796) and even to lead it into some quite out-of-the-way tonal paths, but modern listeners may feel that he did not quite succeed in reconciling the nature of the instrument with the melodic character of the music. Grace Williams showed a fine understanding of how to write lyrically for the trumpet, but in the concerto she solved the problem of the slow movement by placing the main thematic burden in the accompaniment, usually in the bass. The form is that of a passacaglia, and it seems to have been the only occasion in her entire output on which she employed this ancient structure.[9] The passacaglia theme itself, which was briefly and faintly foreshadowed in the *Processional* for orchestra, is particularly interesting for the way it combines a simple repetitive rhythm (suggesting a slow dance) with an extremely sophisticated pitch structure encompassing all twelve notes of the chromatic scale (ex.20). In view of this last feature it is also

Ex. 20

fascinating to observe that the theme is constructed according to principles observed by the strictest serial composers. Bars 3—4, it will be seen, form an exact inversion of bars 1—2 (discounting the last two notes in each case). In more detail, the theme is constructed from a single four-note figure played four times (twice in inverted form), each statement being separated from the next by the same upward step of a tone (= diminished 3rd).[10] It should be noted, too, that the melody pivots on two tritonal axes: C—F sharp ('tonic') defined by the first notes in each bar, and A—E flat ('dominant') by the fourth notes in each bar. The theme's dodecaphony and its symmetrical construction are particularly surprising in view of Grace Williams's known aversion to Schoenbergian techniques, but there is, of course, nothing serial in the way the rest of the music is constructed. The nature of the passacaglia theme does not even tempt her to employ all possible transpositions as Alan Rawsthorne did in the slow movement (*Chaconne*) of his First Piano Concerto. Instead she presents fourteen variations of (or rather on, under, and around) the theme, all at the original pitch. In variations 7 and 8, and again in nos. 10—12, the theme is transferred to an upper part, but it is never played by the trumpet. This sustains a freely declamatory role, suggesting at times the bugle calls of the composer's childhood and at other times a doleful *marwnad* ('lament').

The finale is a simple rondo (A—B—A—C—A). Less original in style and conception than the other two movements, and with a larger amount of exact or near-exact recapitulation, it nevertheless introduces a welcome element of solo virtuosity into the concerto.

9.   The second of the Three Nocturnes for two pianos (1953) is called *Passacaglia,* but in this case the title does not define the structure; the piece was originally called *Phantasmagoria.*

10. It is possible to identify two further statements of the figure, overlapping these; they are shown in ex.20 by dotted brackets.

Next to the trumpet Grace Williams's particular favourites among orchestral instruments were the oboe and its larger brother, the cor anglais, and it was the first of these that she chose for the solo part when in 1965 she was invited to write a 'light-weight, entertaining work' for the BBC in Wales. The result, *Carillons*, is among her most relaxed and delightful inspirations, standing in relation to the larger and more seriously intentioned orchestral works rather as Strauss's late Oboe Concerto stands in relation to his early and weighty symphonic poems. Indeed, the flowing chromatic lines of Strauss's work are occasionally recalled in the first two movements of *Carillons*, as also is its deft, lightly etched scoring. But omission of orchestral woodwind from *Carillons* and the inclusion of bell-like instruments (triangle, glockenspiel, celesta, and occasionally tubular bells) produce an entirely distinctive orchestral palette. It is from the bell-like sounds in the orchestral part that the work gets its title.

Carillons was originally conceived (and performed) in three movements: a short ternary Moderato (A—B—A), with the melody of the first section considerably ornamented on its return, as in a Baroque da capo aria; a delicately scored Allegretto in the style of a pavan; and an Allegro scherzando in a neat, modestly proportioned sonata form. Perhaps its most interesting constructional feature is the unusually direct and fundamental role played by tonality, a role which hinges on the opposition of two tonal centres, B flat and E, separated by a tritone. This tonal axis operates over the work as a whole as well as over separate movements and even individual themes. The two outer movements are in B flat and the central pavan is in E minor (ending however in G, an arm of the 'dominant' C sharp—G axis). The central section of the ternary first movement is in E major, the surrounding sections being firmly in B flat, and E major is again chosen for the recapitulation of the second subject in the last movement. How the same tritonal relationship impinges on the small-scale structure is exemplified by the harmonies that support the opening melody of the work (ex.21; two introductory bars are here omitted).

Ex. 21

In 1973 Grace Williams revised the work, making few alterations to the existing movements but writing an additional one to improve the overall proportions and enliven the element of soloistic display. This takes the form of an accompanied cadenza, whimsically shifting between the rhapsodic and the mercurial and linking the second movement to the last. (Strauss, it will be remembered, had placed an accompanied cadenza at the corresponding place in his Oboe Concerto.) In its final form *Carillons* remains a lightweight work, but with its classical poise and balance it occupies a unique place among Grace Williams's compositions. Its appeal is direct and uncomplicated, but it results from the utmost subtlety and refinement.

Solo songs and opera

It could be argued that the orchestral music constitutes the most consistently successful part of Grace Williams's output, but it was in the solo song, more than anything else, that her musical personality found natural expression. Melody in the widest sense provided the initial impulse for all her compositions, no matter what the medium, and it was her habit to sing a score as she composed it. Moreover, song writing spanned the whole of her career. Her earliest extant composition is a setting of Ben Jonson's *Slow, slow, fresh fount*, written at the age of about 19, and at the end of her life song writing continued to occupy her, even after she had ceased to accept commissions for orchestral works.

In view of this predilection for song writing it is strange to find that between 1939 and 1949 Grace Williams wrote no songs at all (none, at least, has survived). Nearly all the songs she wrote before 1939, when the music of Mahler and Strauss was a potent influence, had orchestral accompaniments, like many of theirs; some of these have been described in earlier chapters.[11] When she returned to song writing in 1949, after her temporary 'retirement' from composition, she began to favour piano accompaniments, and only one song after that date is orchestral. The four that can be assigned to the years 1949−55 (i.e. to the years immediately preceding those at present under review) are all with piano. Of these *Flight* (1949; words by Laurence Whistler) is a difficult but remarkably fine song, its florid, triadically contoured lines recalling some of Britten's early vocal writing (for example the first song in *On This Island*, 1937). It was one of the composer's own favourites, but *To Death* (1953; words by Caroline Southey) is perhaps finer still. Its vocal writing and piano accompaniment (mostly in octaves) are far less demanding but the utterance is more personal, especially in the falling phrases with which each strophe ends (ex.22, overleaf).

Except for the *Two Psalms* for soprano and chamber orchestra (1927), all the songs written before 1958 appeared separately.[12] In 1958, following the orchestral and choral suites of the preceding years, came the first song cycle, *Six Poems by Gerard Manley Hopkins* for contralto and string sextet, written for the Cheltenham Festival. Composers

11. See pages 13−14.

12. It is sometimes possible in the earlier songs to discern an intended grouping which remains unfinalized. For example, *Tuscany* and *Tarantella* (both for mezzo-soprano and orchestra and both composed in June 1930) seem to belong together; and so do *Stand forth, Seithenin* and *Thou art the One Truth* (both for baritone and orchestra, dating from September−October 1935).

49

Ex. 22

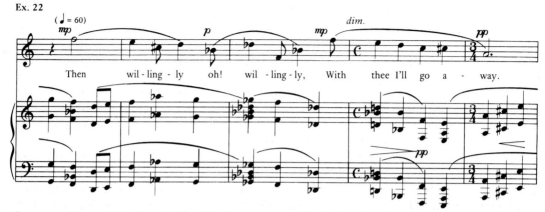

have on the whole found Hopkins's poetry, with its involved syntax and imagery, its internal assonances, alliterations, and half rhymes, and its archaic and arcane vocabulary, peculiarly resistant to musical setting. (Interestingly enough, one of the relatively few composers to respond to its challenge was Grace Williams's teacher, Egon Wellesz, whose setting of *The Leaden Echo and the Golden Echo* was made in 1944.) To appreciate the difficulties one needs only to look at the opening lines of *The Windhover*, the last song in Grace Williams's cycle; these are hard enough to grasp at a leisurely reading, let alone in a setting which aims above all to suggest the pace and exhilaration of a kestrel in flight:

> I caught this morning morning's minion, king-
> dom of daylight's dauphin, dapple-dawn-drawn Falcon, in his riding
> Of the rolling level, underneath him steady air, and striding
> High there, how he rung upon the rein of a wimpling wing
> In his ecstasy!

Possibly Grace Williams did not quite succeed with this one, and in fact she later withdrew it. But why she should at the same time have withdrawn the first song, *Pied Beauty*, is difficult to understand, since the way she accommodates the verbal contrasts of

> With swift, slow; sweet, sour; a-dazzle, dim;
> He fathers-forth whose beauty is past change

within a disarmingly fresh and direct lyricism might well be considered one of the supreme achievements of the whole work. Certainly the cycle would be weakened by the omission of this song, and the suave, muted simplicity of *Peace*, which follows it, would be less effective. Similarly, *Hurrahing in Harvest* (no.5) is less affirmative as an ending to the cycle than *The Windhover*. *No worst, there is none* (no.4) is an impassioned, declamatory setting of an agonizing text, its vehemence unparalleled in Grace Williams's earlier vocal music; and *Spring and Fall* (no.3), with its judicious mingling of *arco* and *pizzicato* brings a welcome touch of textural variety to the string sextet scoring, the lack of which elsewhere might be considered the only serious weakness of this remarkably fine work. A version for string orchestra was planned but was apparently never made.

Neither of the two cycles that followed attained quite the distinction of the Hopkins settings, but they were no less adventurous in the choice of accompanying instruments. The three *Songs of Sleep* (1959) express an untroubled tranquillity, to which alto flute and harp supply an aptly reticent background. Possibly the best song of the group is the last one, a setting of Tennyson's *Sweet and Low* which successfully dispels memories of Joseph Barnby's sentimental partsong. Ten years later the composer included it in another cycle, *The Billows of the Sea*. Another unusual, perhaps unique combination of instruments, harp and harpsichord, is employed in *Four Mediaeval Welsh Poems* for contralto, written for a BBC Festival of Welsh Music in 1962. These are related in structure and in their declamatory vocal style to the orchestral *Penillion* and *Ballads*, and through them to the most ancient traditions of *canu gyda'r tannau*. Three of them (nos.1, 2, and 4) use a stanzaic structure similar to that of the orchestral works, in which an introductory melody (not a folktune, but having something of the character of one) is repeated by the two instruments while the text is sung in a free quasi-improvisatory manner. The first is a lament, the second a nursery song, and the last a setting of 16th-century words:

> There are cuckoos under the trees of the grove
> And if I can sleep in their downy feathers
> As God lives, as far as I know, I shall be happy.
> But if I cannot I shall die.

The third song, *Boddi Maes Gwyddno*, is the longest of the four and has a more complex structure, which is still strophic, but with greater variation in the accompanimental material and a more adventurous tonal range. Grace Williams had set Lady Charlotte Guest's English translation of these words for baritone and orchestra in 1935 as *Stand forth, Seithenin*.

For her final song cycle, commissioned by the Guild for the Promotion of Welsh Music for the 1969 Swansea Festival, Grace Williams returned to a subject (the sea) and a poetic form (the ballad) in which she had shown a special interest all her life. *The Billows of the Sea* was composed for Helen Watts, a singer closely associated with her music, and it contains many passages obviously written with the rich, dark lower range of her contralto voice in mind. It is the only song cycle with piano accompaniment. The musical style is more sophisticated and expansive than one might expect in vocal ballads, and the accompaniment in the first song, *Rosabelle* (Walter Scott), seems to demand orchestral realization for its full effect. The opening is interesting in presenting an archetypal version of a phrase commonly present in the more nationalistic of Grace Williams's later works, although the words are, of course, Scottish (ex.23). Of the other songs *The Lowlands of Holland* is the most folklike, with a clearly strophic form, and *Sweet and Low* is a transposed version of the last of the *Songs of Sleep* (see above) with its original accompaniment for alto flute and harp skilfully, but not very idiomatically, laid out for the piano.

To some extent Grace Williams's songs already reveal her potential as an opera composer in their perfect matching of music and text and in the lively response they show to the dramatic and lyrical possibilities of a poem. What remains untested is her ability to combine both these elements in an extended dramatic framework and to make music

Ex. 23

enhance the delineation of character. For compelling evidence of these gifts it was necessary to wait until 1966, when the composer's only opera, *The Parlour*, was produced in Cardiff by the Welsh National Opera. Grace Williams was by then 60 years old, and it came as something of a revelation to critics and audiences alike that a composer who had spent so long in an operatic backwater, and who had never before attempted an opera herself, should write for the stage with such flair. They would probably have wondered less if they had been more aware of her life-long passion for opera, of her wide and intimate knowledge of the operatic repertory, of her stage work with the girls of Camden High School, and of the music she had written for films and radio plays (particularly *Rataplan*, which had been planned originally as a one-act opera). For many years she had cherished the ambition to write an opera; only the opportunity had been lacking. Even so, *The Parlour* was a noteworthy and unexpected artistic success. Rarely has a composer's first opera turned out so well; even more rarely has such a good first opera remained without a successor.

Admiration for Grace Williams's achievements in *The Parlour* begins with the libretto, which she adapted herself from the short story *En famille* by Guy de Maupassant. Indeed it begins even before this, for to have recognized the dramatic possibilities of Maupassant's story was in itself an indication of a sure dramatic instinct; it was chosen after Tennyson's *The Lady of Shalott* and Vernon Lee's *Dionea* had been considered and rejected as possible subjects. The adaptation itself is masterly. The setting is transferred from France to the living room of a house in a Victorian seaside town, and the action unfolds during the course of a summer's day in 1870. The music is continuous.

Scene 1:   From the open window Grandmamma (contralto) is hurling abuse at the neighbours. Her daughter-in-law (mezzo-soprano) remonstrates with her and Grandmamma retires to her upstairs room in her usual ill temper. Mamma muses on her careful, humdrum life and makes no attempt to hide her indignation when her husband (tenor) comes home with the news that he has been passed over again for promotion at the Navigation Office where he works. Their teenage daughters, Louisa and Augusta (sopranos), return from the harbour, where they have spent the morning. When Grandmamma fails to answer the dinner gong Louisa is sent upstairs to investigate and returns with the news that Grandmamma is lying 'flat on the floor'. Dr. Charlton is sent for and after a hasty examination pronounces her dead. While the two girls go to the post office with a telegram for Aunt Genevieve and Uncle Steve, Mamma, finding that her mother-in-law has left no will, persuades Papa to exchange Grandmamma's superior furniture for theirs before Genevieve has the chance to claim it for herself. Papa wonders what his boss will say when he fails to turn up at the office that afternoon, but he decides that a death in the family is good enough reason to be absent without notice and begins to do as his wife asks.

During the entr'acte, set in the street outside, the neighbours hear of Grandmamma's death and arrange to present their condolences at 7 o'clock that evening. Chimes in the orchestra represent the passing of time.

Scene 2:   While the neighbours share in the family's grief, Louisa and Augusta enter and go up to Grandmamma's room. Later, when they ask why the furniture has been changed, Papa is evasive and Mamma annoyed. While Rosalie, the maid, goes in search of oil for the lamp, the daughters are sent upstairs again ('since they are not afraid') for a candle. They return with the startling news that Grandmamma is getting up and is coming downstairs. Her 'death' was merely a coma, through which she could hear everything. Her reappearance coincides with the arrival of Aunt Genevieve (contralto) and Uncle Steve (tenor), who take Grandmamma's part. Soon Dr. Charlton arrives with the undertaker, and Grandmamma decides that it is time she made a will. All her treasures will go to her daughter Genevieve. Informed by Augusta and Louisa of the latest turn of events, the neighbours arrive to see what is going on and soon find themselves on former terms with their old enemy. Grandmamma gets rid of them, says goodbye to Genevieve and Steve, instructs Papa to return her furniture immediately, and retires to bed. As Papa struggles with a sofa he suddenly reflects: what will he say to his boss now?

Grace Williams found the essential outline of the plot, and many of the details too, in Maupassant's short story, but she had to invent the dialogue, which shows a keen wit, and to fill out the characterization. At the same time she added in many places a new dramatic edge to the narrative. It is in its sharp observation of family relationships and tensions that the libretto of *The Parlour* differs most from that of Puccini's *Gianni Schicchi*, with whose plot there are obvious parallels. *The Parlour* contains no love interest and consequently no aria like the sentimental and very popular 'O mio babbino caro' in *Gianni Schicchi*. Possibly the absence of a comparable 'show-stopper' is a weak point when it comes to popular acceptance, but Grace Williams's unsentimental approach is unquestionably truer to life. As a title *The Parlour* suggests something altogether too cosy.

If the plot puts one in mind of *Gianni Schicchi*, the characterization and to some extent the musical style owe even more to the example of Britten's comedy, *Albert Herring*, another Maupassant story transferred to an English setting. There is, for instance, something of Britten's Lady Billows in the cantankerous old Grandmamma, although Grace Williams's character is rather more venomous, less imperious than Britten's (and a contralto, while Britten's is a soprano). Similarly the daughters, Louisa and Augusta, are in some ways an amalgamation of Emmy and Cis in *Albert Herring* and the nieces in *Peter Grimes*; they usually sing (as they think) together, and their high-pitched, girlish voices lend a distinctive and vivacious vocal colour to the music when they appear. Dr. Charlton, for whom there is no counterpart in the Britten opera, is a much more rounded character than Maupassant's Monsieur Chenet, and a rich source of comedy. Some critics have argued that his failure to diagnose Grandmamma's coma rendered the whole plot incredible,[13] but there are enough well documented instances of similar medical incompetence for an audience to accept it, especially in comedy. Moreover, Grace Williams's Dr. Charlton is not merely incompetent, but perhaps something of an imposter too; at all events he has a 'shady history' and even his name suggests that he is a charlatan.

As in the greatest comic operas, the main strength of *The Parlour* lies in its ensembles. The episode at the lunch table, with Dr. Charlton doing his best to make the girls giggle while their parents react in different ways to the shock of Grandmamma's 'death', is a supreme example of this, and one that shows a true insight into the seemingly callous behaviour that bereaved relatives can show on such occasions. Passages of lyrical expansion are less called for, but Mamma's 'We've not grown wealthy by our labours' and Papa's 'I can't help remembering' (both in scene 1) help to bring those characters to life and are welcome for the expressive contrast they bring to the music. They also invite speculation on what Grace Williams might have achieved with a full-scale serious libretto.

Grandmamma's feud with the neighbours is mentioned only briefly in Maupassant's story, and it would have been quite possible to make an operatic version which did not use a chorus. Indeed it could be argued that to have kept the action 'in the family' would have emphasized the cloistered consanguinity from which the tensions of the comedy spring. But the chorus in *The Parlour* is never allowed to become a dramatic embarrassment, and their entrances and exits (a challenge even to the most experienced opera composer) are managed with unusual conviction. Their music, however, is possibly a little too ambitious in passages where the action is moving swiftly. Much of it proved extremely difficult in pitch and ensemble, even to the WNO chorus, especially in the entr'acte when the neighbours excitedly discuss the news of Grandmamma's seizure.

13. See Arthur Jacobs's review in *Opera*, xvii (1966), 507 – 8.

The Parlour begins and ends in C major. Other keys are chosen for their appropriateness to the expressive or dramatic moment: for example Dr. Charlton's breezy arrival in scene 1 is in a bright D major, and the music associated with Grandmamma's 'death' is largely in B flat minor (the key of the Funeral March in Chopin's Piano Sonata op.35, which is alluded to more than once). But for the most part the music is on the move from one tonal centre to another in a way which is totally in keeping with the pace of the drama; even the set pieces tend to begin and end in different keys, an exception being the neighbours' mock-serious F minor Elegy in scene 2. As far as melodic organization is concerned, one notices no elaborate system of leitmotifs or 'clue themes'; but Grandmamma, whose forceful personality dominates the entire action, is associated with a figure (x in ex.24) which is heard at the very opening of the piece and which constantly reminds us of her presence even when she is off stage.

Ex. 24

The Parlour is without doubt one of Grace Williams's best works, but despite the almost unanimous critical acclaim it enjoyed, popular support was slow in coming; operatic double bills, except for the ever-popular '*Cav* and *Pag*', have never met with much success, it seems. After three seasons in Cardiff and performances in Llandudno and London *The Parlour* was dropped from the WNO's repertory, and it has not been revived since except for four performances by the semi-professional Abbey Opera Group at the Mary Abbott's Theatre, Kensington, in April 1974, when it shared an evening with Darius Milhaud's *Trois opéras minutes*. It is to be regretted that the composer never followed it up with a full-length opera. A television opera was in fact commissioned by the BBC after the production of *The Parlour* in 1966; this was to be produced by Cedric Messina. Grace Williams was eager to do another Maupassant story, *Boule de Suif*, but the BBC production team was not sympathetic to the idea. Balzac's *El verdugo*, Vercors's *Le silence de la mer*, and a fantasy by Marcel Aymé were also considered, but the project was eventually dropped. Ideas for an oratorio to words by Vivien Cutting also came to nothing.

Choral music

For many people the name of Grace Williams is associated primarily with vocal music, and certainly one would expect a composer living in Wales in the first half of the 20th century to find in the voice (and more particularly in massed voices) a natural and convenient means of expression. But, as we have seen, the number of choral pieces she wrote before she was 50 was surprisingly small. Her real interest in choral writing did not begin until 1951, with *The Dancers*, and even after that date it took second place to orchestral music until the last six years of her life. There are in fact only five substantial choral works to be considered in the present chapter, three secular and two sacred.

The earliest of the these is the suite *All Seasons shall be Sweet*, commissioned by the Welsh region of the BBC and completed in 1959. This can be seen in many ways as a successor to *The Dancers*; the vocal forces are identical (soprano solo and women's chorus in three parts) and so is the orchestration except that flute, oboe, and clarinet are added to the strings and harp of the earlier work. The score was published with piano instead of orchestral accompaniment and the work has been performed and broadcast in that version, but for its best effect the original instrumentation is essential. The first of the nine songs is a setting of words by Coleridge in which a mother prays that her child may find that 'all seasons shall be sweet to thee'. It is not a lullaby, but the tender feelings of the mother for her sleeping babe are effectively conveyed in the lulling 5/8 metre and the gently oscillating harmonies of the accompaniment (ex.25). The alternation of tonic with

Ex. 25

flattened supertonic here—the so-called 'Neapolitan' relationship—is often present in Grace Williams's music and is a particular feature of this work. It is prominent again in the fourth and ninth songs.

The songs that follow review the seasons of the year from spring to winter. Spring is represented by two major-key settings of Blake, the first a riot of birdsong (especially in the solo voice and the woodwind instruments), the second reflecting a joyous, laughing innocence. The two summer songs, also in major keys, are settings of the famous lines beginning 'I know a bank' in Shakespeare's *A Midsummer Night's Dream* and Thomas

Heywood's *To Phoebus*, the first for solo soprano and the other for choir. Another Heywood poem, *To Ceres*, tells of harvest time, and two minor-key settings of words by James Thomson and Shakespeare ('When icicles hang by the wall') advance the seasons to winter. Stanzas from Robert Southwell's *Times go by turns* serve as an *envoi*, the key of D major, the irregular metre (a gently pulsating 7/8), and the Neapolitan oscillations all recalling the opening song. The music, like nature herself, has come full circle.

Carmina avium ('Songs of birds'), dating from 1967, is a setting of three Latin texts, the first and last by medieval poets and the second by Catullus; the first is addressed to a thrush, the second tells of a beloved's pet sparrow, and the third is a lament of a swan. Perhaps because the work was composed for the first Cardiff Festival of 20th-century Music, Grace Williams seems here to have deliberately cultivated a more 'advanced' style than she normally and naturally employed at this time. The use of Latin texts is important in this regard, since it encourages a more impersonal approach to word-setting, and it is significant that this was in fact the first time that the composer had set Latin words.[14] The result was a work which in many points of style recalls the middle and late periods of Stravinsky's music: the word-setting is predominantly syllabic and, except for a brief passage between figures 6 and 7 in the first song, entirely and strictly homophonic; there are frequent and unpredictable changes of metre and time signature, particularly in the second song; and the accompaniment is unusually spare, even ascetic, often in only two widely spaced parts. Triadic harmony is not discarded but it no longer governs the shaping of the vocal lines, and unprepared dissonance is freely used. The novelty of Grace Williams's style and vocabulary in this work can best be gauged by comparing the passages already quoted from *The Dancers* (see exx.10 and 11) and *All Seasons shall be Sweet* (see ex.25) with the opening bars of 'Dulci turdule', the first of the *Carmina avium* (ex.26, overleaf).

Carmina avium has received fewer performances than Grace Williams's other choral pieces of comparable size, partly because its rhythms and intervals present a formidable challenge to the singers and also because its original accompanying instruments (viola d'amore and harp) are not easily available to most choral societies. An ordinary viola can be substituted for the first of these instruments and a piano for both of them, but the piano accompaniment is not really satisfactory and it is awkward to play. More approachable in every way is *Ye Highlands and ye Lowlands* for male voices (TTBB) and piano. This was commissioned by the Barry Male Voice Choir in 1972 and, rather surprisingly perhaps, it was Grace Williams's only work for male choir except for a single much earlier song, *Sleep at Sea*. As in *Carmina avium* there are three songs, the first and last being examples of the composer's preferred poetic form, the ballad. The first, whose opening words give the work its title, is the anonymous *The Bonny Earl of Murray*, an elegy in the style of a funeral march. The sombre key (B flat minor), the steady tread of the bass, and the dotted rhythms in the accompaniment are all somewhat reminiscent of the chorus 'Denn alles Fleisch es ist wie Gras' in Brahms's *Ein deutsches Requiem* (a work Grace

---

14. The *Two Psalms* for soprano and chamber orchestra (1927) have Latin titles, but the words are in English. So are those of the *Benedicite* (1964).

Williams disliked), but the melodic lines are wholly characteristic of the composer, with frequent use of that rhythm for which the term 'Scotch snap' is for once appropriate. Next comes a love-song to well-known words by Robert Burns; the contrast it makes with the first song is emphasized by a key (E major) as far removed from it as possible. Walter Scott's *Jock of Hazeldean*, the final song, is given a suitably vivacious setting in F sharp major, with a hint of Shostakovich in the hornpipe-like piano refrain and in the way that a 5/8 bar is occasionally inserted into the strongly metrical 2/4 melody (ex.27). The resource and skill with which Grace Williams matched the strophic form of the ballad while avoiding any hint of repetitiousness are as much to be admired here as in orchestral works such as *Penillion* and *Ballads*. The least satisfactory aspect of *Ye Highlands and ye Lowlands* is the piano accompaniment, which seems to have been conceived as an orchestral short score. It is, however, more playable than that of *Carmina avium*.

Sacred choral music occupies a relatively small part of Grace Williams's output, the only two works of any importance being the *Benedicite* and the *Missa Cambrensis*. It is

relevant to mention in this connexion that she was not herself a believer or a regular church-goer. As far as religious doctrine goes she was an agnostic and the moral philosophy by which she lived was, if anything, humanism. She did, however, acknowledge Christianity as a force for good and a source of virtue, and she cherished its culture and traditions, as many agnostics do. In 1970 she wrote to her friend Vivien Cutting: 'If there is anything decent about me it's the result of my Christian heritage so how can I deny I'm a Christian?'[15] If allegiance without belief is acceptable to the Godhead, then Grace Williams's sacred works entail no dissembling; in any case, she was not the first non-believer to set the Creed to music.

The *Benedicite* was written for the Montgomeryshire Secondary Schools' Choir and Orchestra to perform at the 1965 Royal National Eisteddfod in Newtown, and the circumstances of that performance determined both the scoring and the character of the music. The choral writing is in two parts only, soprano and alto (with, however, frequent divisions; a version for mixed choir followed later), and the orchestral scoring is expertly

15.   Grace Williams to Vivien Cutting, 16 March 1970.

tailored to non-professional forces while offering a challenge to young players. The harmonic texture is unusually diatonic, encouraging a confident manner in performance that accords well with the nature of the text. This brings the style of the music closer to that of Vaughan Williams than is usual at this period, and the work shows certain superficial resemblances to that composer's setting of the same text. Both works include one solo part, for soprano, and both are in the key of D major. There are, on the other hand, important differences between the versions of the text used by the two composers. Vaughan Williams omits many of the repeated phrases ('praise him and magnify him for ever') and incorporates a hymn *Hark, my Soul* by J. Austin; Grace Williams uses the opening of *The Song of the Three*, 'Blessed art Thou, O Lord God of our Fathers' (not in the prayer-book version), for an imposing *maestoso* introduction and closes with the doxology, which Vaughan Williams omits.

It is not merely these textual differences, however, that result in Grace Williams's setting being a work of more ample proportions than her teacher's. Her setting achieves its greater length through a fuller working-out of each line of the text, involving suitable representation in the music of all the manifestations of Creation ('Winter and Summer', 'Frost and Cold', 'Lightnings and Clouds') contained in this great hymn of praise. The work falls into twelve sections, some of them separated by brief pauses, whose variety of tempo, metre, and tonality more than compensate for any monotony that over-exposure to one kind of vocal timbre might produce. Because of its conservative harmonic idiom the *Benedicite* is perhaps the least representative of all Grace Williams's later works, but in its four-part version it would repay the attention of any enterprising choral society.

Towering over all the other choral works is the *Missa Cambrensis*, composed for the 1971 Llandaff Festival and inscribed to the memory of her friend Nancy Elizabeth Jenkins, who died of cancer shortly before the work was completed. Among all Grace Williams's works only *The Parlour* exceeds it in scale and duration, and it took over two years to compose, from late 1968 until March 1971. It was the composer's last large-scale work and it can be regarded in many ways as the consummation of her life's work.

No other composition gives such eloquent evidence of the high regard in which Grace Williams held the music of Benjamin Britten. The idea of incorporating non-liturgical material into the Latin rite is one that stems directly from Britten's *War Requiem* (1962), while other features reminiscent of Britten's work include the use of a distant boys' choir, the sound of bells (particularly in the Credo and Sanctus), and the predominance in some passages of the C−F sharp tritone. Also reminiscent of the *War Requiem*, but adumbrated in Grace Williams's own music as well, are the sinuous chromatic lines and the quintuplet groupings of the opening Kyrie. With its suggestion of contained power this section makes an impressive opening to the work. 'Kyrie eleison' is sung by the choir, a pedal C underpinning their imploratory chromatic lines (ex.28); the trumpet's characteristic quintuplet figure is then taken up by the four soloists for 'Christe eleison', after which varied repeats of both imprecations result in an arch-like structure with the climax firmly placed at the centre (five bars after figure 6).

After the quiet, resigned ending of the Kyrie, the opening of the Gloria brings the greatest possible contrast with its high-pitched choral sound and its ebullient, even fren-

Ex. 28

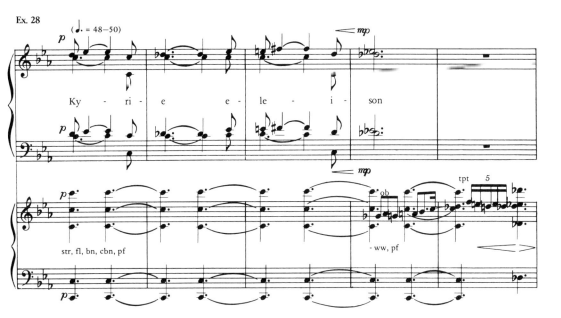

zied rhythms — bars of 5/8, 7/16 etc breaking up the basic 6/8 metre. Unlike the other movements, the Gloria is divided into distinct subsections differentiated by tonality, tempo, and scoring, and separated by brief pauses. The six subsections are:

1. Gloria in excelsis: C major, Vivo (chorus)
2. Laudamus te: B flat major, Larghetto (soloists and chorus)
3. Domine Deus: G major, Allegro moderato (chorus)
4. Qui tollis: E flat major, Poco lento (soloists)
5. Quoniam tu solus sanctus: transition passage (Più mosso) mostly for solo voices, leading to
6. Cum sancto spiritu: C major, Moderato con moto (chorus).

This suggests a structure altogether more fragmented than is in fact the case, since the key of each section is prepared by the ending of the previous one and consistent use of the mode of alternate tones and semitones (found in other movements as well) lends homogeneity to the harmonic texture. One of the most attractive and memorable sections is 'Domine Deus', notable for the lilting inequality of the metre (5 + 3 semiquavers to the bar), the graceful interweaving of the lithe chromatic lines, and the delicate scoring (see the facsimile facing page 63). Once again the style recalls Britten (for example the *Cantata misericordium* of 1963) but the confidence and freshness of the music make it easy to ignore any indebtedness. Indeed it would be a mistake to place too much importance on Britten's influence on the work as a whole. It is undoubtedly present, but the

Composer's autograph, with conductor's annotations, of the beginning of 'Domine Deus' from the *Missa Cambrensis*.

music is stylistically consistent with other works of the period and Grace Williams's personality is stamped on every page.

If the level of inspiration and craftsmanship in these first two sections were maintained throughout the mass we should be dealing here with one of the masterpieces of 20th-century British choral music. But in the remaining sections one is forced to acknowledge some falling off. To begin with, the two extra-liturgical interpolations in the Credo fail to achieve what was evidently intended, or at best elicit an ambivalent response. They were designed in the first place to separate 'et homo factus est' from 'crucifixus'[16] and also to give the work a particular relevance to Wales. The first is the Welsh Christmas carol (*Carol Nadolig*, words by Saunders Lewis) that Grace Williams had composed in 1955, and this is sung here by the boys' choir, lightly accompanied by a distant ensemble of viola, cello, and harp. But although textually appropriate at this point its effect is distracting, and this is true also of the reading in Welsh of the Beatitudes, in which the narrator's lines are punctuated by phrases on the strings and oboe. The interpolations fail mainly because the music is feeble in comparison with the rest of the work and because they are not essential to its conception in the way that the Owen poems are essential to Britten's conception in the *War Requiem*. Their omission could easily be effected[17] and would greatly improve the overall shape of the section.

More fundamentally damaging to the shape of the work as a whole is the preponderance of slow tempos after the Gloria. Only for one or two brief passages (including a short recapitulation of some of the Gloria music in the Agnus Dei) does the speed exceed a steady Moderato, and for most of the time it is a good deal slower. This is partly because of Grace Williams's unorthodox but strongly held views on the nature of the Creed:

> I'm not feeling it as the usual downright affirmation . . . As I feel it 'Credo in unum Deum' is about the most mystical thing of all.[18]

Her mysticism is expressed in long sustained F sharp octaves alternating in wind and strings, with the intoning of the choir, punctuated by glockenspiel and bell, adding an aura of ritual. But the predominantly slow tempo does not mean that the music is without interest. Even while respecting the oldest traditions of mass composition Grace Williams can find ways of refreshing its conventions, as is shown by her treatment of 'descendit de coelis'. A downwards scale is employed, as it usually is, but this time it is one of alter-

16. 'I've always been puzzled by the nativity being followed immediately by the crucifixion' (Grace Williams to Vivien Cutting, n.d. [December 1969]).

17. Perhaps by proceeding from the seventh bar after figure 9 to figure 1 after the carol, and making another cut from the beginning of the Beatitudes to the beginning of 'Crucifixus'.

18. Grace Williams to Vivien Cutting, 9 May 1969.

nating tones and semitones, characteristic both of the composer and of the work, and it makes its descent over almost three octaves, through the entire range of the solo voices (ex.29). 'Et resurrexit' is set to an ascending form of the same scale, beginning quietly and

Ex. 29

molto misterioso — a moment of awesome contemplation quite different from the jubilant affirmation with which Bach and Beethoven, among others, expressed the text at this point.

Grace Williams treats the Sanctus and Benedictus as a single section. The setting of the Sanctus itself is rich in contrasts: between a solo boy treble and unison chorus for the opening phrases; between wind and strings for the accompaniment to this antiphony; and between the statuesque tempo for these exchanges and the warmer, livelier movement of 'Hosanna in excelsis'. The Benedictus brings some of the most relaxed and melodically attractive music in the work; it is based on material from the orchestral *Processional* of 1962, another Llandaff Festival piece. The transition from its gentle G major tonality to the troubled C sharp minor of the final section, the Agnus Dei, is a supremely dramatic moment (ex.30).

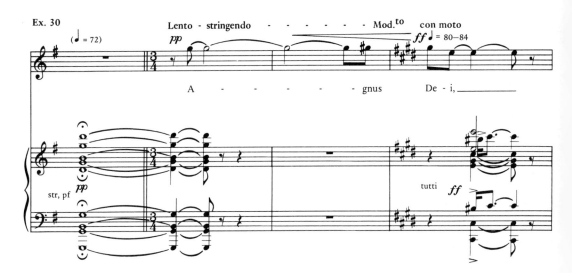

Ex. 30

Up to now (1980) the *Missa Cambrensis* has been heard only once, in a performance which did nothing to minimize the formidable challenge it presents, above all to the choral singers. It may not be an unflawed masterpiece, but it is a work of great power, rich in incident, generous in feeling, and exemplary in craftsmanship. Its continued neglect is something that ought to prick the consciences of all Welsh choral societies.

V THE LAST YEARS : 1972–1977

One thing I hate: being called a veteran[1]

The *Missa Cambrensis* was the last of Grace Williams's large-scale works. By the time it was performed she had reached the age of 65, and the years that remained to her may be regarded nominally as a period of retirement, at least to the extent that she resolved after the Mass not to accept further commissions. Pressing requests made it impossible for her to fulfil this resolve to the letter, but at least she could agree to write only those works which she would have written anyway. Her rejection of other commissions, for example for orchestral works, was prompted also by a very real concern that younger composers in Wales should benefit instead of her from the kind of support she had enjoyed from the BBC and the Arts Council. It was made possible by a measure, not of affluence — a condition she would have spurned — but at least of financial security.

> I've never felt so well off because not having had much time during my freelance years — or the inclination — to go out and spend simply for spending's sake, my savings have sort of mounted up . . . and I contributed to a pensions scheme from which I draw £3 p.w. less tax and the ever-increasing O.A.P. [old-age pension] and royalties on performance etc. so I have no money worries . . . Of course I'm not what most people today would call well-off but it's ample for me.[2]

Retirement brought the opportunity for further revision of earlier compositions and doubtless for the destruction of some that had escaped previous bouts of self-criticism, or self-doubt. But it also brought the chance to write the kind of music, particularly solo songs, that the composer most wanted to write but which circumstances had hitherto forced her to neglect. The harvest of these last years is not large, but the music is on the whole of superb quality and in many ways of particular interest. It may reveal little of the 'philosophic mind' that we experience in the late works of Beethoven or Bach; nor is it tinged with autumnal feelings of farewell like the last-period compositions of Strauss and Mahler. In fact it would be misleading to speak at all of a 'last period' in Grace Williams's music if by that we meant a radical departure from the style or expression of the earlier music. But it is perhaps not too fanciful to recognize in the works of these last years, which are without exception vocal works, a certain quality of reflection; they seem to suggest that the composer has lived for a long time with the poems she sets and thought deeply about them.

Four works claim particular attention, two for solo voice and two for choir. The first is *Fairest of Stars*, a setting for soprano and orchestra of words from Book 5 of Milton's

---

1. Grace Williams to Gerald Cockshott, 11 March 1976.

2. Grace Williams to Vivien Cutting, 12 December 1974.

Paradise Lost, written in 1973 for a recording of Grace Williams's music made by EMI under the auspices of the Welsh Arts Council;[3] the first public performances followed in February 1974. The words form an invocation to all Creation to praise the Maker of all things: the sun, moon, air, rain, winds, birds, fish, and 'ye that walk / The earth, and stately tread, or lowly creep' are called upon in turn to sing His praise. (The order closely follows Genesis, i.) It is in fact a kind of Benedicite, but the musical response is quite different from that of the *Benedicite* that Grace Williams wrote in 1964. *Fairest of Stars* was her first aria for solo voice and orchestra since the 1930s and its style recalls the chromaticism and the rich orchestral textures that characterize the music of those years. As the voice soars and sweeps in ecstatic arches of melody it is easy to lose sight of the words and to picture some Sophie or Arabella in the grip of a more secular passion (ex.31). Even more Straussian is the singer's final phrase (ex.32). As is often the case in

Ex. 31

3. HMV, ASD 3006.

Ex. 32

Strauss's vocal music, the thematic thread of *Fairest of Stars* is drawn mainly by the orchestra, but the overall structure is determined by the irregular stanzaic construction of Milton's verse. The orchestral passages separating each stanza recall material from the seven-bar introduction, which is in turn reminiscent of the opening of the Sanctus from the *Missa Cambrensis* and of 'Rosabelle' from *The Billows of the Sea*. Not every listener will be able to respond sympathetically to music which seems more in tune with the world of 1913 than with that of 1973; most will find it difficult to resist its sensuous appeal and impossible not to admire its technical mastery.

Ex.31, above, serves also to illustrate a technical feature of *Fairest of Stars* which is common to all the important works of this late period: the widespread employment of the mode of alternate tones and semitones (at 'His praise' and in the preceding oboe scale). The slightly different but no less characteristic mode used in the preceding vocal phrase will be described in the next chapter. Both modes are used extensively in the *a cappella* setting of the ancient Marian hymn *Ave maris stella*, possibly the most impressive work of this period. The first three words of the hymn, 'Ave maris stella' ('Hail, star of the sea'), form a refrain, and its supple phrases, suggesting the soft swell of the sea, contrast with the mainly syllabic, homophonic, and more squarely rhythmic setting of the verses. This alternation of flowing refrain with more rigidly and concisely organized verses (the contrast extends to tempo as well) is maintained for the first four stanzas, after which the refrain recedes, like an ebb-tide, leaving its imprint on the final quiet amens. As well as being among the finest of all Grace Williams's choral works this is also the most taxing, its rhythms and intervals presenting insuperable difficulties to all but the most accomplished and intrepid singers (ex.33; note again the mode of alternate tones and semitones).

To write *Ave maris stella* for the 1973 North Wales Music Festival, Grace Williams had to break her resolve not to accept further commissions, but it is nevertheless possible to

discern a strong personal impulse behind the music. Similarly, the idea of setting Robert Browning's dramatic monologue *My Last Duchess* had been in her mind at least since 1960, but the immediate incentive to writing it was a request in 1974 from the Jewish baritone, Louis Berkman, for a new work to include in a Purcell Room recital the following March. *My Last Duchess* is not an obvious candidate for musical treatment, but it is possibly one of the least prolix of Browning's poems. An Italian duke shows the portrait of his late wife to the emissary of the count whose daughter he is about to marry, revealing as he does so the duchess's goodness, his own heartlessness, and the conflict between the two that led to her cruel end. In 1960 Grace Williams had contemplated adapting Browning's poem as a short stage work in collaboration with Vivien Cutting. The project had to be shelved because work on *The Parlour* had just begun, and it was never taken up again in that form. But the straightforward setting for baritone and piano that eventually materialized does call for some measure of dramatic presentation. On the score it is described as a scena, and in a note the singer is at one point advised to stand 'with a distant, haunted look in his eyes'. It seems to have been intended that he should also use mime to suggest the presence of the emissary and of the duchess's portrait. The composer's main interest, however, was in the character of the duke himself, whom she she apparently saw as ruthless and cruel but not altogether insensitive to his wife's virtues. The work gives some indication of what Grace Williams might have achieved as a composer of serious opera; even the piano accompaniment seems to have been conceived in orchestral rather than keyboard terms.

It was fitting that for her very last composition (at least as far as her complete and extant works are concerned) Grace Williams should return for inspiration to the sea, and her setting of two interlinked choruses to words by Rudyard Kipling and Thomas Lovell Beddoes shows no falling-off in her ability to write evocative sea music and to respond imaginatively to the imagery of poetic texts. Indeed there is about this music a new adventurousness, not least in the unusual scoring of the accompaniment for two horns and harp (the same instruments that Brahms used to accompany his *Vier Gesänge* for women's voices, op.17). It was a brilliant idea to bring together these two poems, which complement each other in a variety of ways. In the first chorus, *Harp Song of the Dane Women*, only the sopranos and contraltos sing Kipling's words, the tenors and basses suggesting the swell of the sea in wordless lines which the composer suggests, with a touch of irony perhaps, should be vocalised to the vowel 'o', as in 'shore'. The effect of the women's mournful song against (or more often in alternation with) the discrete but menacing sea music is haunting and deeply expressive (ex.34). In the second chorus, *To Sea! To Sea!*, the roles are reversed, the men voicing Beddoes's rousing call of the sea and the women for the most part joining with the instruments in evoking its restless motions and moods. Like *Ave maris stella* these choruses require singers of exceptional ability, and for this reason, and because there can be no substitute for the unusual and demanding instrumental parts, they have not so far entered the choral repertory. A gramophone recording which included this work and *Ave maris stella* would do Grace Williams's reputation an immense service.

The two interlinked choruses (to which Grace Williams never, unfortunately, gave a collective title) received their first performance in St. Augustine's Church, Penarth, on 28 February 1976, as part of that year's BBC St. David's Festival. Just nine days earlier the composer had celebrated her 70th birthday, an event which brought many tributes from the musical world as well as celebratory performances of several of her works throughout Wales. A 70th-birthday concert by the BBC Welsh Symphony Orchestra included the recently completed revised version of the Second Symphony. Official honours had come her way during the preceding decade, including the John Edwards Memorial Award from the Guild for the Promotion of Welsh Music for *The Parlour* and offers of an OBE in 1966 and of a Civil List pension in 1969. These two she declined, and even her closest friends and relatives were unaware of them until after her death. A good performance of one of her pieces meant more to her than a decoration, and the appearance on disc of some of her major orchestral works brought her deep satisfaction during her last years.[4]

The first intimations of what was to prove a fatal cancer came in May 1976, just as Grace Williams was about to leave Barry for one of her now infrequent visits to relatives. Hospital treatment during the autumn, which included drugs, radiotherapy, and an operation, left her debilitated and afforded no permanent improvement in her condition. She bore both the disease and its treatment bravely, but composition was impossible. Her courage during these last painful months, something of which can be gauged from what she fails to say in her letters to friends, was matched by her calm acceptance when it became clear that recovery was impossible. On 25 January 1977 she wrote a moving letter of farewell to her lifelong friend Elizabeth Maconchy:

> Since I wrote I'm afraid there have been developments in my illness and now I know the therapy failed and there's nothing they can do except ease it as much as possible.
> I've been in a very nice small hospital for ten days or so, with all my friends at hand, and now Marian [the composer's sister] is here (having had leave of absence from her teaching job) indefinitely. If the nursing becomes too much for her I can return to the nice hospital.

4.   For details see Appendix II.

Ex.34

What is a wo-man that you for - sake her, and the hearth-fire ____ and the home a - cre,

To go with the old grey wi - dow-ma-ker?

Well, all along I've known this could happen and now it has I'm quite calm and prepared and can only count my blessings — that I've had such a run of good health — able to go on writing — and just being me with my thoughts and ideas and sensitivity. It's not what's happened to me, but that I've had the great good fortune to be able to respond to so many wonderful things. From now on it won't be so good but even so there are sunsets and the sea and the understanding of friends — and a marvellous broadcast of Solti's recording of Meistersinger on Sunday.

Our friendship has been one of my rarest and most precious blessings. I've believed in your genius ever since our college days . . . Would you let Dorrie [Dorothy Gow] know? and thank her for — well for being just Dorrie — so compassionate and courageous and having that lovely sense of humour. You were both so kind to me when I first came to the college and had a great influence for good on me . . .

When the end comes it will be just close family at the crematorium and family flowers only. I've always hated funerals and for long have determined not to inflict mine on others . . .

When the end did come, just over a fortnight later on 10 February 1977, Wales lost a selfless, courageous woman, and one of its finest composers.

VI PERSONALITY AND STYLE

I am and have always been a romantic[1]

In outward appearance there was nothing at all remarkable about Grace Williams. A quiet, well-spoken lady with a slightly shy but welcoming manner, neatly but not ostentatiously dressed: this is how she might have seemed to anyone meeting her for the first time, at least in her later years. If the meeting took place at her home in Barry the visitor might also have noticed the modesty of her surroundings, the plain furnishings (among which a 19th-century Broadwood grand piano, formerly her father's instrument, would attract most attention), the unpatterned walls hung with reproductions of her favourite Vlamincks, and the cleanliness and good order that everywhere prevailed. Here, the visitor might have thought, is a creative artist to whom household chores are no burden, and he might even have been given the benefit of a few precepts on how to organize the spring-cleaning, on the right way to vacuum a carpet (slowly and deliberately), or on the value of housework as a means of combining domestic economy with the first stages of musical creativity.

If these first impressions suggested someone of ordinary gifts and conventional outlook, they were soon contradicted by her conversation. To talk with Grace Williams was a rewarding experience for a musician, no matter how frustrating it might be for the interviewer who had come along to learn something about her own music. Reluctant to say much about this, she would soon divert the conversation towards some topic on which her enthusiasm could be allowed free rein: Verdi's *Don Carlos*, perhaps, or Wagner, or the wizardry of Berlioz's orchestration. She was always more ready to discuss the music of younger Welsh composers (several of whom owed a great deal to her personal interest and encouragement) than to talk about her own, and she was not slow to temper her enthusiasm with words of condemnation if she thought a particular work merited them, or if she considered a composer to be compromising his own artistic ideals and potential. Both in conversation and in her voluminous correspondence she was never malicious in her forthright expressions of opinion, but she would have nothing to do with that kind of 'discretion' that results only from pusillanimity. She was herself sensitive to criticism but never for long resentful of it.

Often her conversation would range beyond music to the books she had recently read or to the plays and films she had seen. All her life she was a keen theatre-goer and a devoted radio listener, and in her later years television became a favourite source of relaxation. She was extremely well read, and although she would never parade her knowledge one soon became aware of her wide and deep acquaintance with English and

1. Grace Williams to Gerald Cockshott, 30 November 1947.

French literature. Discussion of a *Carmen* production, for instance, would be conducted not only with precise references to Bizet's score but with a close understanding of Mérimée as well. Her own gifts as a writer are evident in her many BBC scripts, the libretto of *The Parlour*, and her copious letters. A natural modesty does not altogether explain her reluctance to bring a conversation back to her own music, for her letters show without any doubt that the misgivings she felt about its true value troubled her deeply. Incredible as it might seem to friends and colleagues, there were times when, like Mahler, she doubted the worth of anything she had composed, and while this self-questioning never resulted in despair or in the drying-up of the creative urge, it does help to account for the constant revision to which she subjected many of her scores and the complete destruction of others.

To many people who knew her Grace Williams must have seemed a lonely person, especially after the death of her mother in 1962. Her decision to forego the joys and satisfactions of marriage and motherhood and to look for fulfilment as a composer must, one suspects, have cost a great deal to someone whose personal relationships were so warm and whose love of children was spontaneous and genuine. It is not surprising that much of this warmth and tenderness was transmuted into music; what is perhaps surprising is that she seems never to have become embittered by the self-denial her decision must have cost her, even when visited by misgivings about her art. There had been one or two romantic friendships during her student days, and in the early years of the war she formed a close attachment with a member of a Polish community working at a factory in Grantham. Together with colleagues from Camden High School she was invited to teach English to some of the Poles, and it was in this way that she became aquainted with Zen Sliwinski. He was about the same age as she was, but although they had much in common he was not a musician and seems to have been jealous of the place that music took in Grace Williams's life. Certainly it was largely at his insistence that she temporarily gave up composing after her illness in the 1940's:

> If *he* hadn't taken himself off to S. Africa I shd. never have had the misfortune to return to composing. I shd. have had more respect for myself if I'd died of a broken heart but alas, a few days after he'd gone I began to feel free again. Life is very rum — but he was very wise.[2]

In the summer of 1970 Zen Sliwinski unexpectedly turned up in Barry on his way to visit his native Poland for the first time since before the war, and he called in at Barry a second time on his return journey to Cape Town. It requires little reading between the lines of Grace Williams's letters to realise how much it meant to her to see him again, but her final comments on the incident serve to place the whole relationship, and perhaps others too, in perspective:

> I'm not going to rationalise any more about Zen's visit; all I know is that it was good to see him restored once more to his former Polish-ness when he returned from Poland . . . He came here to tell me all about it and soon produced a bottle of cherry brandy (in memory of some celebration we had during the war — in Lincs!) and we filled two

2. Grace Williams to Gerald Cockshott, n.d. (? April 1950).

glasses and drank to our past . . . He said he'd be back to see me next Summer but goodness knows. Anyway, it seems to have acted as a shot in my writing arm — and I've felt quite happy copying away for hours at a stretch . . . All my (non-composer) friends think it was a lovely thing to happen to me after all these years of being shut up alone with my composing — but I've no regrets. I got a lot from knowing him — he taught me tolerance . . . yet there were whole areas of my life he didn't belong to — and vice versa.[3]

The friendship with Zen was woven into Grace Williams's music with the *Polish Polka* (1948), based on a traditional tune which he had brought to her attention.

The composer Daniel Jones, whose music Grace Williams greatly admired and to whom she was for many years indebted for long and penetrating analyses of her scores, was convinced that her compulsive letter-writing was evidence of her extreme loneliness.[4] This may well be true, but her enormous correspondence seems to have had its source also in a mild but deep-seated agoraphobia. Childhood holidays away from home had been painful to her and, while she later became less prone to homesickness and was able to travel quite widely without ill effect, a disastrous holiday in Yugoslavia in 1951 revived the condition. Letter writing became to some extent a substitute for the visits to friends and relations that she felt it increasingly impossible to make. Her surviving letters run into many hundreds, possibly thousands. They deal extensively and interestingly with the composition and performance of many of her major works and are also full of illuminating comments on other music. Particularly important on this level is the correspondence with her fellow composer, Elizabeth Maconchy, which also furnishes glimpses, as do letters to other intimate friends, of the personality behind the music. Above all they reveal the deep concern she felt for other people. Foremost in her thoughts when writing a letter was the welfare of the recipient, and words of sympathy, advice, and encouragement are never stinted. The letters also convey a profound social conscience — a sense of fellowship with the oppressed, the deprived, and the unfortunate, whether victims of apartheid in South Africa, the underprivileged of the 'Third World', or the sufferers and mourners in the Aberfan disaster nearer home. Left-wing radicalism she saw as offering the best hope of social justice, and pacifism the brightest prospects for world peace or, if not that, at least the most honourable course for the individual.

For Grace Williams art and life were not things apart, and her warm humanity is unmistakably present in the music. A striking instance of personal experience transmuted into music is provided by her reaction to the disaster at the South Wales mining village of Aberfan in 1966, when a pit-heap collapsed and engulfed the village school, causing the deaths of nearly 150 children. The composer was at the time at work on her portion of the *Severn Bridge Variations*, a collaborative work by three English and three Welsh composers to commemorate the opening of the suspension bridge linking Gloucestershire and Monmouthshire across the River Severn.

3. Grace Williams to Vivien Cutting, 17 August 1970.

4. 'Grace Williams: a Symposium (Part Two)', *Welsh Music*, v/7 (1977 – 8), 41 – 2.

> When I heard the Aberfan news I just couldn't take it in — and sat down to work as usual and wrote my piece and it wasn't until I'd finished the score . . . that I got the full impact of the disaster — and then realised that subconsciously it was all in the music.[5]

Grace Williams's variation comes fifth in the set; it takes the form of a chorale prelude in the style of an elegy.

Generosity, companionableness, tolerance, wisdom, modesty, independence of mind: these are some of the qualities that those who knew Grace Williams best remember in her. But the one attribute that she possessed in full measure, and that shines through all her other qualities, was integrity. It was something that governed her whole life and art. At a mundane but nonetheless important level it formed the basis of her commercial dealings and of the professionalism with which she conducted her affairs. In money matters she was scrupulously honest, almost to a fault. Vivien Cutting has described how, on a visit to Paris together in the 1930s, Grace Williams would sit up in bed at midnight 'working out the exact amount in centimes she owed me for the day';[6] and when in 1967 a confusion over names and titles brought her a substantial but unearned cheque from the Performing Rights Society she refused to accept it, despite assurances from the Society that the mistake was theirs and that they had funds to cover such errors. Where matters of principle or artistic judgment were concerned there could be no compromise, and commissions were accepted only if she felt a creative urge strong enough to fulfil them to her satisfaction. Vivien Cutting has summed up what must have been the experience of many:

> I think those . . . who knew Grace at all intimately must feel that through her they learnt the full meaning of the word 'integrity'.[7]

Integrity is a quality stamped on Grace Williams's music as much as on her personality; indeed it makes the two inseparable. First acquaintance with the music is therefore likely to arouse similar impressions to those experienced on first acquaintance with the composer herself, and it would be easy for a modern listener to dismiss it as conservative, and even provincial. Conservative it certainly is, in the context of mid-century European stylistic developments, but closer familiarity soon reveals a distinct personality which to recognize is to value highly.

The roots of Grace Williams's style may be sought in the music she particularly admired during her formative years. Wagner was an early passion, and a somewhat surprising one for a young person at that time; she herself considered *Tristan und Isolde* to have influenced her more than any other work of art. The Wagnerian experience is already reflected in her earliest extant composition, *To Night*, written as a degree 'exercise' in 1925 – 6; here, however, it is to *Die Walküre* rather than to *Tristan* that the composer seems principally indebted (ex.35).

5.   Grace Williams to Vivien Cutting, 3 November 1966.

6.   'Grace Williams: a Symposium (Part Two), *Welsh Music*, v/7 (1977 – 8), 50.

7.   *Ibid.*

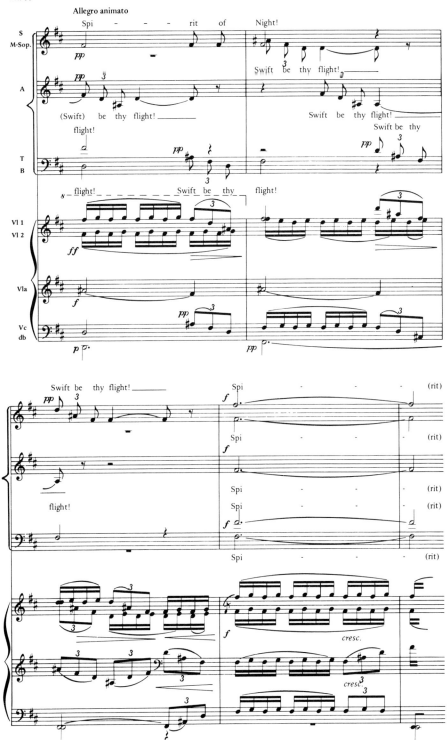

Soon her interests extended to post-Wagnerians such as Strauss and, after her sojourn in Vienna in 1930–31, Mahler. (Her enthusiasm for Mahler's music, probably fostered by her friendship with Britten in the 1930s, must have seemed even odder to her contemporaries than her liking for Wagner.) Vaughan Williams was a figure whose influence younger British composers, even if they were not his own pupils, could hardly avoid in the period between the two World Wars, but Grace Williams's receptivity to British music also embraced that of Walton and, more importantly, Britten. Shostakovich was another admired composer whose influence is occasionally perceptible. Her interest in 20th-century music did not, of course, stop with Britten and Shostakovich, but although she took an open-minded interest in the aleatory and electronic techniques of the younger generation she never found them relevant to her own music.

It is in the harmonic idiom she cultivated that Grace Williams's conservatism is most apparent. No matter how Romantically expressive her music may be, and no matter how complex its aggregation of chromaticism in the form of passing notes, suspensions, appoggiaturas, and so on, a strong gravitation towards the triad is nearly always present. Not infrequently a passage of apparently complex harmonic texture is reducible to a succession of straightforward triads. The main theme of the slow movement of the Sinfonia Concertante furnishes a good example of this. For all the opulence of its sound (see the extract quoted at ex.5) it consists essentially of no more than a series of triads related to each other only in the sense that each one has at least one note in common with the next (ex.36; see also ex.39). Two recurrent features of Grace Williams's harmony are the

Ex. 36

alternation of two chords, often forming a 'Neapolitan' relationship (see exx.1, 10, 21 and 25), and the non-functional use of the 'dominant' 7th (see exx.21, 23, 31 and 34). The latter is common enough in the music of Strauss, as well as in that of Debussy, Fauré, and others.

The proliferation of diatonic and chromatic unessential notes tends to impose on a good deal of Grace Williams's middle-period music (i.e. that written between c1936 and 1955) a slow rate of harmonic change. When a slow harmonic rhythm goes hand in hand with a leisurely metronomic tempo, and even more when the harmonic framework consists of tonally unrelated chords (as in ex.36), the music runs the risk of losing its momentum. In some contexts this may matter very little; one is content, for example, to drift along with the last of the Sea Sketches, entitled 'Calm Sea in Summer'. But sometimes a prolonged aimlessness in the harmonic flow can be disconcerting to the listener, and in the end crippling to the music's vitality. Characteristic of the period is the absence of key signatures and the lack of a basic tonal centre for a piece, or even a movement. It would be quite misleading to call the music 'atonal', since by atonality is understood a freely chromatic idiom without the kind of hierachy implicit in the triad and its derivations. To the extent that triads imply keys, Grace Williams's music is never atonal, but in the works she wrote during the 1930s and 1940s tonality is often extremely elusive. Extended pedal points frequently serve to engender some sense of key at crucial points in the structure.

Among the stylistic changes that took place in the music composed after 1954 was a new approach to tonality — a reaffirmation of its effectiveness as a structural agent. After that date tonal centres are usually more firmly established and more stably maintained, operating to shape an entire work as well as individual movements and sections. Key signatures begin to appear regularly again. When this new feeling for tonality coincides with features that can be identified as nationalistic in origin the result is often a more diatonic harmonic idiom, but this does not mean that the chromaticism of the earlier style is completely forsaken. On the contrary, at least one source of that chromaticism — the use of non-diatonic modes or scales — becomes even more prominent in the later music. One such mode is shown in ex.37; beginning on the note C, its pitches are

Ex. 37

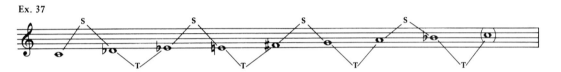

separated by alternate tones (T) and semitones (S). The regular alternation of these two intervals means that the mode can exist only at this or two other pitches (a semitone higher or lower), since whichever note is taken as a starting point the succeeding notes will always be the same as in one of these three cases. (Each of the twelve different transpositions of the major or minor scale, by contrast, has the same succession of intervals but a different succession of pitches.) Ex.37 is, in fact, called by the composer Olivier Messiaen a 'mode of limited transposition' (the second such mode in his personal system),[8] but it is doubtful whether Messiaen's theoretical system or his own music had anything to do with Grace Williams's adoption of it. A more likely source of her interest in the mode would be the music of Bartók; Ernö Lendvai identified it as the 'basic scale' in what he described as Bartók's 'chromatic system'.[9] But it seems just as probable that the mode was simply 'in the air' at a time when composers were looking for alternatives to, or refinements of, the major — minor system. Several English composers, including Walton and Britten, have used it; so, too, have a number of Welshmen, including David Harries, Alun Hoddinott, Daniel Jones, and William Mathias.

Some instances of this mode can be seen at exx.29, 31, 33 and 34. Its salient features, as far as Grace Williams's music is concerned, are: (1) the flattened 'supertonic', encouraging those 'Neapolitan' progressions which have already been mentioned as a

8.   O. Messiaen: *The Technique of my Musical Language* (American translation, Paris, 1944), 59 – 60.

9.   E. Lendvai: *Béla Bartók: an Analysis of his Music* (English edition, 1971), 51ff.

feature of her harmonic style; (2) the sharpened 4th and flattened 7th, which lend a 'modal' flavour (in the traditional sense) to many of her melodies; and (3) the inclusion of both major and minor 3rds (E flat and E natural in the above example), which are often brought into proximity or even simultaneity in her music to piquant effect. All these features are present also in another eight-note mode shown at ex.38. This differs from the

Ex. 38

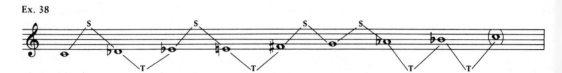

one at ex.37 in only one note (A flat instead of A natural) but this is enough to break the symmetry and to make all transpositions possible. It is perhaps even more widely used in Grace Williams's music than the other, and is more personal to her. Instances of its use are found in most periods of her creative life, but it is particularly prevalent in the later works, notably in the two interlinked choruses to words by Kipling and Beddoes. Either of the two modes can lend an elusive quality to the music and they are frequently employed in conjunction with the direction *misterioso*, which appears as frequently as *liricamente* in her scores.

In view of the importance that Grace Williams attached to melody ('she invariably sang everything she wrote, vocal or instrumental, as she went along'),[10] it may seem strange to suggest that harmony rather than melody was fundamental to her musical thinking. But insofar as it is possible to separate the two, it does seem that her melodies are shaped by the harmony rather than the other way round. There is, for example, as A. F. Leighton Thomas has pointed out, a tendency to form melodies around the notes of a triad.[11] Instances may be seen at exx.6, 10, 11 and 34, above; the opening theme of the Violin Concerto (1950) provides a more extended example (ex.39). This extract also serves to

Ex.39

10.   Elizabeth Maconchy in 'Grace Williams: a Symposium', *Welsh Music*, v/6 (1977), 18.

11.   A. F. Leighton Thomas: 'The Music of Grace Williams', *Anglo-Welsh Review*, xv (1965), 99.

illustrate the broad, wide-ranging melodic lines typical of the middle-period works. Such writing is not entirely absent from the later music too (and *liricamente* remains a favourite mark of expression), but to a considerable extent it is replaced, from *Penillion* (1955) onwards, by a new, very different, and more original kind of melody which has been aptly labelled 'declamatory'.[12] Its contours are less dependent on the underlying harmony, which is often static, and it is characterized by short phrases, usually occupying a narrow range, separated from each other by rests or by long-held notes. Certain rhythmic figures are usually stamped on the melody by repetition. Among these might be a triplet of repeated notes immediately preceding a strong beat, or a quintuplet semi-quaver group; probably the commonest is the 'Lombard' rhythm in association with a rising 2nd or other interval on an accented beat (usually the first of a bar). Some melodies of this type have already been quoted (see exx.12−14, 19, 23 and 28); ex.40 shows an archetypal one from *Castell Caernarfon* (1969).

Ex. 40

It is in works with obvious Welsh connexions *(Penillion, Castell Caernarfon; Four Mediaeval Welsh Poems, Missa Cambrensis)* or in which a specifically Welsh feeling is intended (Trumpet Concerto, *Ballads for Orchestra, Processional)* that the declamatory style is most in evidence. Whether or not the average Welsh concert-goer would recognize

12. *Ibid*, p.96.

it, Grace Williams came closer in these works than any other Welsh composer has done to achieving a musical style which was at once contemporary, individual, and nationalistic. It would take a Welshman thoroughly conversant with the language and with the oldest traditions in Welsh literature to determine the extent to which this style truly reflects the rhythms and cadences of the language and the moods of its ancient legends. But that it should do this seems to have been the composer's intention:

> I had a thorough grounding in Welsh airs and Welsh folk songs when I was a child and teenager, and they found their way into some very early works, now withdrawn, and of course into the *Fantasia*. Then later on in the fifties there was the influence of the rhythms, intonations and cadences of Welsh oratory, and the atmosphere of the Mabinogion, which can be felt in my *Penillion* for Orchestra. Later still, I've done some settings of medieval Welsh poetry which I think are very Welsh. Indeed I've always considered myself very fortunate to have been born Welsh.[13]

That Grace Williams should relate her nationalistic style to Welsh oratory and literature rather than to folksong invites one to draw parallels with Janáček's aims in Czechoslovakia earlier in the century. At the same time it is interesting to observe that some stylistic features are present in transcriptions made from the oldest source of Welsh instrumental music, the ap Huw manuscript (ex.41; note especially the 'Lombard' rising 2nd, called in the manuscript *y Plethiad byr*).

Ex. 41
Slow

Ap Huw MS, p.62; transcribed P. Crossley-Holland, *Music and Letters*, xxiii (1942), 151

Grace Williams's habit of singing what she wrote has already been mentioned, and in view of this practice it is surprising how angular her melody lines could be, even in vocal music. Her Viennese training may have had something to do with this, since wide and 'awkward' leaps are a feature also of the early works of Schoenberg and of the music of Mahler, among others, but the scarcity of extant scores from those years makes it difficult to be certain about this. Octave leaps enliven the melodic contours from the very beginning, and leaps of even wider intervals are quite common. These are less characteristic of the 'declamatory' melodic style, but they are by no means absent from the later vocal music. Nor are they confined to solo lines, as is shown by the quite typical extract from the first song of *All Seasons shall be Sweet* at ex.42.

Counterpoint of a formal kind is almost completely absent from Grace Williams's music. Except in the last movement of her BMus composition, *To Night*, she wrote nothing that might be called a fugue, and there are few and only brief passages of strict canon in her work. But in her orchestral music, particularly of the pre-1955 period, there

---

13.   A. J. Heward Rees: 'Views and Revisions', *Welsh Music*, v/4 (1976 − 7), 18.

Ex.42

Whether the sum-mer clothe the ge-ne-ral earth With green-ness,— or the

red-breast sit and sing— Be-twixt the tufts of snow on the bare branch Of mos-sy

ap-ple-tree,— while the nigh thatch Smokes in the sun-thaw

is a tendency towards a proliferation of free counterpoint in middle parts, reminiscent of Wagner and Strauss, which the composer often found it necessary to keep in check. The chamber-music textures of, for example, the *Sea Sketches* are heard as the contrapuntal elaboration of a harmonic progression; counterpoint in the sense of adding melody to melody is more the province of the 'declamatory' Welsh works.

Just as strict contrapuntal devices and closed contrapuntal forms were foreign to Grace Williams's nature as a composer, so, it could be argued, were Classical symphonic forms. Sonata form, even in the broadest sense of something stated, developed, and restated, was confined almost entirely to her early and middle-period works, and genres traditionally associated with sonata structures are almost completely absent from her mature output. The only exceptions are the Second Symphony and the Trumpet Concerto, but the first of these, even if it can be included among her most successful works, leaves one with the impression that the composer has responded to symphonic form as a challenge rather than turned to it as the natural vehicle for what she wished to express. The Trumpet Concerto represents her most successful attempt to contain within Classical structures a musical imagination that found its most congenial expression in poetic or narrative forms — in song and suite rather than in symphony and sonata. It is a second opera, not a third symphony, that one would most like Grace Williams to have written.

Rhythm is not a constituent of Grace Williams's style that attracts immediate attention or calls for much discussion. In this department her music shares very little common ground with the mainstream of 20th-century composition represented by Stravinsky and Bartók, for example, or even by Shostakovich and Hindemith. But this is not to say that rhythm is unimportant to her music. In her early years she enjoyed dancing as a form of relaxation, and among her first works were two ballet scores. Both the march and the dance are frequently encountered in her music; *alla marcia* and *marciale* are favourite designations for a movement and titles often reflect a dance origin (e.g. *Polish Polka, Hornpipe: Keel and Anchor, Rondo for Dancing, The Dancers*). Violent, insistent, and percussive rhythms are on the whole foreign to her style but her manipulation of metre can be extremely subtle, and the seemingly effortless and flexible rhythmic flow of much of the music is often the carefully calculated result of using irregular time signatures such as 5/4 and 7/8 or of making frequent changes of metre, sometimes from bar to bar.

More distinctive perhaps is Grace Williams's orchestration. She usually wrote for a full orchestra of Romantic proportions, with double woodwind (and such 'extras' as piccolo, cor anglais, bass clarinet, and double bassoon), four horns, two trumpets, three trombones, the usual strings, and a large selection of percussion instruments. Rarely did she experiment with large *ad hoc* ensembles, but the Trumpet Concerto omits orchestral trumpets and *Carillons* includes no woodwind apart from the solo oboe. No previous Welsh composer had scored for the modern symphony orchestra with such skill and individuality. Her fondness for the trumpet and her wholly distinctive way of writing for it have already been mentioned, and it is the trumpet writing more than any other single feature that makes her mature orchestral music immediately recognizable. The oboe and the cor anglais are also prominent in her scores, sometimes as echoes of the trumpet (at the opening of the Trumpet Concerto, for example) but more often with melodic lines fashioned to their distinctive timbres. The harp usually finds a place, too, as one might expect from a composer deeply conscious of her Welsh background, and it is perhaps surprising that she wrote so little solo or chamber music for the instrument. (It does, however, play an important accompanimental role in several solo songs and choral pieces.) In her handling of the orchestral instruments she rarely looked for novelty for its own sake, and while the percussion section may include such exotic instruments as castanets and maracas, they are used sparingly and with precise calculation of their effect. The only 'special effect' for which she showed any predilection in her scores was that of *sul ponticello* tremolandos for the strings, particularly in *misterioso* passages. Her orchestration shows imagination and individuality but it is always practicable, and like her teacher, Vaughan Williams, she frequently suggested alternatives or cued in parts for performances with fewer or different instruments.

It would do Grace Williams's memory no service to exaggerate her importance as a composer, and she herself would have been the first to deplore any tendency to do so. In the geography of Western European music during the 20th century her oeuvre occupies a sheltered backwater, and its ripples have scarcely been felt on the high seas of contemporary art. But in the history of music in Wales she occupies a position of the first importance. Although active as a teacher, it was mainly through personal example that her influence was felt. She showed younger Welsh composers that it was possible (even if it was not easy) to live in Wales as a freelance creative artist; she demonstrated to Welsh musicians the importance of cultivating the highest possible professional standards; she helped to place orchestral music in Wales on a new footing; and she brought to the concert hall for the first time a distinctively Welsh musical language. Above all, she left many works of the highest quality and originality which Welshmen, and not only Welshmen, will do well to cherish and to perform.

APPENDIX I

CATALOGUE OF WORKS AND INDEX

Abbreviations:

A	alto/contralto	OUP	Oxford University Press
arr.	arranged	perc	percussion
attr.	attributed	pf(s)	piano(s)
B	bass (voice)	pubd	published
Bar	baritone	rev.	revised
cl(s)	clarinet(s)	S	soprano
db	double bass	str	string(s)
fl	flute	T	tenor
hn(s)	horn(s)	tpt	trumpet
M-Sop	mezzo-soprano	UWP	University of Wales Press
no(s).	number(s)	vc	violoncello
ob	oboe	vl(s)	violin(s)
orch(d.)	orchestra(ted)	vla	viola

Solo voices are separated by commas (S, A, T etc); choral voices are run on without commas (SATB, TTBB etc).

In each section of this catalogue the arrangement is chronological, as far as possible, except in the last category (Miscellaneous Arrangements) where it is alphabetical. The information is set out under the following headings:

Title (author). Works without title are indicated by square brackets. Texts are English unless otherwise stated. Details of instrumental and vocal scoring are shown where appropriate; a diagonal stroke (/) separates alternative requirements.

Date. This is in most cases the date when the work was completed in score. Undated works are listed alphabetically at the end of each category.

Publication. Publisher and date of publication are shown where applicable. Most works exist only in manuscript (MS), and for these locations are given using the following key:

A   In the possession of Marian Glyn Evans, the composer's sister. Most of these are deposited on loan in the Welsh Music Archive, University College, Cardiff.

B   BBC Music Library, Cardiff.

C   BBC Music Library, London.

D   National Library of Wales, Aberystwyth.

E   In private hands, as indicated.

F   British Library, London

Locations are not shown for MS copies of printed works, and no attempt has been made to distinguish between original MSS and xerox (or other photographic) copies.

Page nos.   These refer to pages in the text where the work is mentioned; music examples are also listed.

STAGE AND INCIDENTAL MUSIC

Title (genre, author)	Date	Publisher	Page nos.
The Dance of the Red Shoes (ballet)	c1933	lost	
Theseus and Ariadne (ballet, Eric Bailey) 1. Ariadne's Dance 2. Entry of Theseus and the Athenians	c1935	MS:A	22
Hannibal (radio play, Robert Gittings)	May 1947	lost	29
Aucassin and Nicolette (radio play, Sam Langdon)	?1948	MS: A (rough pencil score)	
The Dark Island (dramatic poem for radio, Henry Treece)	1948	MS: A	30
Blue Scar (film)	1948	MS: A (parts, and score of Mountain Sequence)	30
The End of a World (dramatic programme for radio, Henry Treece)	1 Jan 1949	MS: A (rough pencil score), B	
Rataplan (radio fantasy, Henry Treece)	1 March— 26 April 1949	MS: A	29,52
David (film)	1951	MS: A (parts)	29,36
The Story of Achievement (film)	1952	MS: A (parts)	
Siwan (radio play, Saunders Lewis)	?1954	MS: A (sketches)	
Letter to Wales (film)	? after 1956	lost	
The Parlour (opera, Grace Williams, after Maupassant)	25 Aug 1961	MS: A	37,52—5, 60,69,70, 74; ex.24
[Commonwealth Festival poetry reading] (incidental music)	?1965	MS: A	
Esther (play, Saunders Lewis)	Jan 1970	MS: A, B	13(n8)

ORCHESTRAL MUSIC *(full orchestra unless otherwise stated)*

Title	Date	Publisher	Page nos.
Overture: Hen Walia	1930	MS: A	18,19,22
Suite for Orchestra	1932	MS: A	

Title (author; scoring)	Date	Publisher	Page nos.
Concert Overture	?c1932	MS: A	
Movement, tpt, chamber orch	1932	MS: A	45(n9)
Suite, chamber orch [see Suite for Nine Instruments under Instrumental and Chamber Music]			
Elegy, str orch	1936, rev. 1940	MS: A	19–23,25, 31; ex.4
Four Illustrations for The Legend of Rhiannon 1. The Conflict 2. The Nuptial Feast 3. The Penance 4. The Return of Pryderi	1939, rev. 1940	MS: A	20,31; ex.9a
Fantasia on Welsh Nursery Tunes	1940	OUP, 1956	22,23,26,36, 82
Sinfonia Concertante, pf, orch	20 June 1941	MS: A	23,24,36,78; exx.5,36
Symphonic Impressions (Symphony no. 1)	7 July 1943	MS: A	20, 24–6, 33,36; ex.6
Sea Sketches, str orch 1. High Wind 2. Sailing Song 3. Channel Sirens 4. Breakers 5. Calm Sea in Summer	1944	OUP, 1951	26,27,33,35, 36,78,83; exx.7,8
Polish Polka [also for 2 pfs]	April 1948	MS: A	75,83
The Merry Minstrel (with narrator)	12 July 1949	MS: A	30
Suite: The Dark Island, str orch 1. Prologue 2. Barcarole 3. Alla marcia 4. Epilogue	Oct – Nov 1949	MS: A	30,33
Violin Concerto	11 Feb 1950	MS: A	21,31–3, 36,80,81; exx.9b, 39
Variations on a Swedish Tune: The Shoemaker, pf, orch	May – June 1950	MS: B	
Hornpipe: Keel and Anchor	11 Sept 1953	MS: A	33,83

Title	Date	Publisher	Page nos.
Seven Scenes for Young Listeners	21 April 1954	MS: A	33,69—71; ex.34
1. The Curtain Rises			
2. The Lazy Swing			
3. The Procession			
4. Street Cries			
5. The Gossiping Puppet			
6. The Princes in the Tower			
7. Final Episode			
Penillion	7 April 1955	OUP, 1962	36,38—43, 51,58,81,82; exx.12—14
Symphony no.2	1956, rev. 1975	MS: A, B	33,37, 42—5,70, 83; exx.17,18
Processional	14 April 1962, rev. 1968	MS: A	45,47,64,81
Trumpet Concerto	29 Nov 1963	MS: A	45—7,81,83, 84; exx.19,20
Carillons, ob, orch	19 Nov 1965, rev. 1973	MS: A	48,49,82; ex.21
Severn Bridge Variations (no. 5)	1966	MS: A	75,76
Ballads for Orchestra	15 April 1968	MS: A	36,41—3, 51,58,81; ex.16
Castell Caernarfon	1969	MS: A	36,41,81; ex.40
Welsh Dances [see under Instrumental and Chamber Music]	?	MS: A	

CHORAL MUSIC

Title (author; scoring)	Date	Publisher	Page nos.
To Night (Shelley; S, M-Sop, A, T, B, chorus, str orch)	1925—6	MS: D	12,33,76, 77,82; ex.35
Gogonedawg Arglwydd/Hymn of Praise (12th-century Black Book of Carmarthen; chorus, orch) [Welsh/English text]	June 1939	MS: A (pencil score)	21,22,33

Title (author; scoring)	Date	Publisher	Page nos.

The Dancers (S, SSA, str orch, harp/pf)
  1. Gather for festival (H.D.)
  2. Tarantella (Belloc)
  3. Roundelay (Chatterton)
  4. Lose the pain in the snow (May Sarton)
  5. To the wild hills (Kathleen Raine)
	Aug — Oct 1951	OUP, 1953	33—6,56,
			57,83;
			exx.10,11

The Flower of Bethlehem/Carol Nadolig (Grace Williams/Saunders Lewis; SATB) [English/Welsh text]	1955	OUP, 1958	63
Sleep at Sea (Christina Rossetti; TTBB, pf)	c1955	MS: A	57
Yr Eos/The Nightingale (Ieuan Ddu/ Grace Williams; SSA, pf) [Welsh/English text]	Dec 1958	UWP, 1960	

All Seasons shall be Sweet (S, SSA,
orch/pf)
  1. All Seasons shall be Sweet (Coleridge)
  2. The Song of Spring (Blake)
  3. When the green woods laugh (Blake)
  4. Midsummer Night (Shakespeare)
  5. To Phoebus (Thomas Heywood)
  6. To Ceres (Heywood)
  7. The Wintry Waste (James Thomson)
  8. When icicles hang by the wall
    (Shakespeare)
  9. Stanzas from *Times go by Turns*
    (Robert Southwell)
	20 Aug 1959	UWP, 1963	56,57,82,83;
			exx.25,42

Hymn to the Earth (Homer, translated by Shelley; unison voices with divisions, pf)	Jan 1962	MS: A	
Benedicite (S, SA/SATB, orch)	30 Sept 1964	MS: A	21,57(n14), 58—60,67

Carmina avium (SATB, vla d'amore/vla,
harp) [Latin text]
  1. Dulci turdule (Julius Caesar Scaliger)
  2. Passer, delicate meae puellae (Catullus)
  3. Ploratione cygni (anon, 9th century)
	17 Feb 1967	MS: A	57,58; ex.26

Can Gwraig y Pysgotwr (John Blackwell [Alun]; SSA, pf/pf duet) [Welsh text]	12 Dec 1969	National Eisteddfod, n.d.	
Missa Cambrensis (Latin Mass, Welsh Bible, Saunders Lewis; S, A, T, B, chorus, boys' choir, orch) [Latin and Welsh text]	11 March 1971	MS: A	37,58,60— 66,68,81; exx.28—30

Title (author; scoring)	Date	Publisher	Page nos.
Ye Highlands and ye Lowlands (TTBB, pf)	1972	MS: A	57—9; ex.27

1. The Bonny Earl of Murray (anon)
2. O my luve's like a red, red rose (Burns)
3. Jock of Hazeldean (Scott)

Ave maris stella (anon; SATB) [Latin text]	2 May 1973	OUP, 1975	68—70; ex.33
[Two interlinked choruses] (SATB, 2 hns, harp)	7 Nov 1975	MS: A	35, 69, 70, 80; ex.34

1. Harp Song of the Dane Women (Kipling)
2. To Sea! To Sea! (T. L. Beddoes)

Three Lyrics (Shakespeare; SSA, pf)	?	OUP, 1959	

1. Sigh no more, ladies
2. Orpheus with his lute
3. Blow, blow thou winter wind

The Burning Babe (Robert Southwell; SA, pf)	?	MS: A	
Psalm 150 (SS, pf) [Welsh text]	?	MS: A	
The Witches' Sabbath (Ben Jonson; SABar, pf)	?	MS: A	

SOLO VOCAL MUSIC

Title (author; scoring)	Date	Publisher	Page nos.
Slow, slow fresh fount (Jonson; voice, pf)	c1925	MS: A	49
[Two Psalms] (S, chamber orch)	1927, rev. c1935	MS: A	13,14,49, 57(n14); ex.1
1. Super flumina (Psalm 137) 2. In convertendo (Psalm 126)			
Slumber Song (Sassoon; voice, fl, vla, harp)	c1928	MS: A	14
They closed her eyes (Masefield; voice, str quartet)	c1928	MS: A	14
Service of All the Dead (D. H. Lawrence; T/S, orch/pf)	c1929	MS: A	14
Tuscany (V. Sackville West; M-Sop, orch)	June 1930	MS: A	49(n12)
Tarantella (Belloc; M-Sop, orch/pf)	June 1930	MS: A	33,49(n12)
I had a little nut tree (traditional; S, orch/pf)	?c1930	MS: A	

Title (author; scoring)	Date	Publisher	Page nos.
Green Rain (Mary Webb; S, orch/pf)	7 Feb 1933	MS: A	
The Mad Maid's Song (Herrick; S, orch/pf)	June 1933, rev. ?	MS: A	
Oh! snatch'd away in beauty's bloom (Byron; T, orch/pf)	20 – 21 Sept 1933	MS: A	
Oh! weep for those that wept (Byron; T, orch/pf)	March 1934	MS: A	
Stand forth, Seithenin (Lady Charlotte Guest, from the Welsh; Bar, orch)	Sept – Oct 1935	MS: A	49(n12),51
Thou art the One Truth (Dhan Ghopal Mukergi; Bar, orch)	Sept – Oct 1935, rev. 1950	MS: A	49(n12)
The Song of Mary (Bible; S, orch)	1939, rev. 1940	MS: A	20–22,28
Fairground (Sam Harrison; T, pf)	1949	MS: A	
Flight (Laurence Whistler; T, pf)	Oct 1949, rev. Sept 1953	MS: A	49
When Thou Dost Dance (anon, 17th century; voice, pf)	Sept 1951	MS: A	
The Lament of the Border Widow (anon; M-Sop, pf)	1952	MS: A	
To Death (Caroline Southey; voice, pf)	Nov 1953	MS: A	49; ex.22
Six Poems by Gerard Manley Hopkins (A, str sextet)	May 1958	MS: A, C	33,49–51

Six Poems by Gerard Manley Hopkins (A, str sextet)
1. Pied Beauty
2. Peace
3. Spring and Fall
4. No worst, there is none
5. Hurrahing in Harvest
6. The Windhover

Songs of Sleep (S, alto fl, harp)	1959	MS: A	51

Songs of Sleep (S, alto fl, harp)
1. Come, sleep, and with thy sweet deceiving (Beaumont and Fletcher)
2. The cypress curtain of the night (Campion)
3. Sweet and Low (Tennyson)

Four Mediaeval Welsh Poems (A, harp, harpsichord) [Welsh texts]	7 Sept 1962	MS: A, B	51,81

Four Mediaeval Welsh Poems (A, harp, harpsichord) [Welsh texts]
1. Stafell Cynddylan (9th century)
2. Hwiangerdd (7th century)
3. Boddi Maes Gwyddno (13th century)
4. Claddu'r Bardd (16th century)

Title (author; scoring)	Date	Publisher	Page nos.
Lights Out (Edward Thomas; T, pf)	1965	MS: A	
Two Ninth-century Welsh Poems (anon; Bar, harp) [Welsh texts] 1. Y Dref Wen 2. Eryr Pengwern	1965	MS: A	
The Ballad of the Trial of Sodom (Vernon Watkins; S, T, tpt, perc, harp)	Aug 1965	MS: A	
Fear no more the heat o' the sun (Shakespeare; voice, pf)	1967	MS: A (pencil score)	
When my love swears (Shakespeare; T, pf)	? 1967	MS: A (pencil sketch)	
The Billows of the Sea (A, pf) 1. Rosabelle (Scott) 2. Sweet and Low (Tennyson) 3. The Lowlands of Holland (anon) 4. Black-eyed Susan (Gay)	Summer 1969	MS: A	51,68; ex.23
Fairest of Stars (Milton; S, orch)	11 August 1973	MS: A	66—8; exx.31,32
My Last Duchess (Browning; Bar, pf)	Oct 1974	MS: A	69
Crys y Mab/The Lover's Shirt (anon, 16th century; S/M-Sop, harp/pf) [Welsh/English text]	?	MS: A	
Mary Stuart to Elizabeth I (Mary Stuart; voice, pf)	?	MS: A (pencil score)	
Ow, Ow, Tlysau (anon, 16th century; T, pf/harp) [Welsh text]	?	MS: A	

INSTRUMENTAL AND CHAMBER MUSIC

Title, scoring	Date	Publisher	Page nos.
Fantasy Quintet, pf, str quartet	c1928	lost	13
Sonata, vl, pf	Nov 1930, rev. Nov 1938	MS: A	15,21
Sextet, ob, tpt, vl, vla, vc, pf	? c1931	MS: A	15,16,21; ex.2
Sonatina, fl, pf	c1931	MS: A	15—17; ex.3
The Silent Pool, pf	? c1932	MS: A	

Title, scoring	Date	Publisher	Page nos.
Suite for nine instruments, fl, cl, tpt, pf, 2 vls, vla, vc, db	c1934	MS: A	16,17
Cavatina, str quartet	? c1937	lost	22
Rhapsody, 2 cls	Aug 1939	MS: A	
Polish Polka, 2 pfs [also for orch]	?	OUP, 1950	75,83
Three Nocturnes, 2 pfs	April 1953	MS: A	47(n9)
1. Serenade			
2. Passacaglia			
3. Masque			
Variation on 'Where's my Little Basket Gone?' (attr. A. Scott-Gatty, orchd. Vaughan Williams) [part of composite work]	1955	F (Add.MS 59809)	
Hiraeth, harp	1957	UWP, 1961	
Yr Helfa, harp	1957	lost	
[Piece for the left hand], pf	1958	MS: A	
Cân Ramantus, hn, harp	1959	MS: E (Miss Ann Griffiths)	
Marwnad Cynddylan, tpt, pf	April 1970	MS	
Rondo for Dancing, 2 vls, vc/db	? c1970	Guild for the Promotion of Welsh Music, n.d. [1976]	83
Romanza, ob, cl	?	MS: A	
Welsh Dances, fl, cl, tpt, 2 vls, vla, vc, db [also for orch with multiple str parts]	?	MS: A	
1. Siencyn's Dance			
2. Bryniau'r Werddon			
3. Maypole Dance			
4. Morris Dance			
5. Jig			
6. Folk Dance			

ARRANGEMENTS FOR SCHOOLS BROADCASTS

Folksong and carol arrangements for the BBC schools programme 'Rhythm and Melody'. All are for voices (mainly unison) and orch. MS: B (unless otherwise indicated), A (some piano scores).

Six carols (broadcast Christmas 1946):
    Ding dong merrily on high; Rocking Carol (Czech); A little child on the earth (Flemish); Patapan; Wassail Song; The Twelve Days of Christmas

Six folksongs (broadcast Easter 1947):
    The Mocking Bird (Appalachian); Annie the Miller's Daughter (Slovak); The Wood-pigeon (Portuguese); The Feng-Yang Drum (Chinese); The Musician (French); My Horses ain't Hungry (Kentucky)

Six carols (broadcast Christmas 1947):
    Susanni; Christmas Song; Sledging; O Little One; The Kingdom; Shepherds in the fields abiding

Five folksongs (broadcast Easter 1948):
    The Keeper; High Barbaree; Time for man go home (West Indies); Carol of Service; Git along little dogies (American)

Three carols (broadcast Christmas 1948):
    Wassail Song; Shepherds watched their flocks (Czech); Down in yon forest (English)

Five folksongs (broadcast Easter 1949):
    The Tailor and the Mouse; Come, mah little darlin' (Negro); Newcastle (orch only); Little red bird (Manx); Spinning Wheel Song (Manx)

Three folksongs (broadcast Summer 1949):
    My bonny cuckoo (Irish); Sing, said the mother (Appalachian); Cradle Song (Czech)

Four folksongs (broadcast Easter 1950):
    O Rare Turpin; The Shepherdess (French); Bonny at Morn; The Song of the Flax (Russian)

Three folksongs (broadcast Summer 1950):
    Bill Bones' Hornpipe; Out in the garden (Swedish); The Derby Ram

Four carols (broadcast Christmas 1950):
    King Herod and the Cock; Today in Bethlehem; Jesus, rest your head; A Merry Christmas

Five folksongs (broadcast Easter 1951):
    A Fairy Lullaby (Gaelic); What say you? (Finnish); Audulko (Czech); Buriano (Bulgarian, orch only); Hark to the millwheels (French)

Two folksongs (broadcast Summer 1951):
    The Wonderful Inn (arr. Brahms, orchd. Grace Williams); The Drummer Boy (French)

Four songs (broadcast Christmas 1951):
    The Mallow Fling (folksong); The Cradle (Austrian carol); Infant Holy (Polish carol); Come, ye lofty (Breton carol)

Four songs (broadcast Easter 1952):
    Tik-tak (Serbian); Lullaby (Stephen Storace); The Cuckoo; Holahi, holaho (German)

Four songs (broadcast Summer 1952):
    Per Spelmann (Norwegian); Robin-a-Thrush; Dorabella (Tchaikovsky); Git along, little dogies

Three songs (broadcast Christmas 1952; MS not in B):
  Sally Anne; Bethlehem calls you (carol); Gloucestershire Wassail (carol)

Four folksongs (broadcast Easter 1953):
  Donkey Riding; Hilo Somebody; Gently Mary; Charlie is my darling

Three songs (broadcast Summer 1953; MS not in B):
  The Meeting of the Waters; Houza (Czech folksong); The Barley Mow

Two songs (broadcast Christmas 1953):
  Kukulienka (Slovakian); Sleep my Little Son (German carol)

Four songs (broadcast Easter 1954; MS not in B):
  Winter has gone (German folksong); The Holly (Welsh folksong); Faithful Johnny (Scottish);
  Oh! 'Twas in the broad Atlantic

Three songs (broadcast Summer 1954; MS not in B):
  Tooralee, Tooralay, Tooralo (Czech); Lullaby (Bernhard Flies); Blow the man down (sea
  shanty)

Also numerous arrangements of Welsh airs for BBC programme 'Cerddi Cymru', MS: A

MISCELLANEOUS ARRANGEMENTS *(listed alphabetically)*

A Lauterbach (Alsatian); voice, pf, MS: A [French text]

Five American Folksongs: Some love coffee, Buinorie, The Two Sisters, The Wisconsin Emigrant,
  The Swapping Song; ob, vl, vc, harp. MS: B, C

The Blackbird; unison voices, pf. OUP 1958

Cadi Ha; SA, pf. Gwynn Publishing Co. 1939 [Welsh/English text]

Cariad Cyntaf; Bar, vla, pf. MS: A [Welsh text].

Dacw 'Nghariad i lawr yn y Berllan/See my love in the orchard yonder; SSA. UWP 1960
  [Welsh/English text]

Four Folksongs: O Rare Turpin, The Shepherdess/Il était une bergère, Bonny at Morn, The Song
  of the Flax; voice/unison voices, pf. OUP 1951 [English/French text: no. 2]

Two French Folksongs: Le Chevalier du Guet/The Cavalier on Patrol, Margoton va-t-à-
  l'eau/Belinda went to the well; voice/? unison voices, pf. OUP 1949 [French/English texts]

The Gentle Dove; unison voices, pf. OUP 1958

Hela Llwynog/Hunting the Fox; SATB. UWP 1959 [Welsh/English text]

Hen Wlad fy Nhadau (melody by James James); Bar, TTBB, orch. MS: A [Welsh text]

The Jolly Pedlar; unison voices, pf. Adam & Charles Black 1955

The Little Princess/Hun Gwenllian; S/S, A, pf/harp. OUP 1958 [English/Welsh text]

The Loom; voice, pf. OUP 1960

The Lovely Dark Maid/Yr Eneth Ffein Ddu; voice, pf. MS: A [English/Welsh text]

Siencyn's Dance; fl, pf. MS: A

Spanish Sailing Song; 2 pfs/orch. MS: A

Squirri-wirri-wip (Norwegian folksong); B, 2 cls, harp, vl, vla, vc. MS: C

Three Traditional Ballads: Sweet Primroses, The Lass of Swansea Town, Fair Lisa; T, fl, ob, str quartet. MS: A (rough pencil score), E (Sir Peter Pears)

Underneath the flowing sea/Dwfn yw'r Môr; T, pf. MS: A [English/Welsh text]

The Vale of Llanberis; S/SA, pf/harp. OUP 1958

Watching the Wheat/Bugeilio'r Gwenith Gwyn; voice, pf. OUP 1952 [English/Welsh text]

[Two Welsh Airs]: Jim Cro/Jim Crow, Hwian Hwi fy Mhlentyn Tlws; voice, pf. MS: A (no. 1 UWP 1936) [Welsh/English texts]

[Two Welsh Airs]: Dafydd y Garreg Wen, Y Bore Glas; voice, pf. MS: A [Welsh texts]

[Two Welsh Airs]: O send to me an apple, Rhosymedre (melody by J. D. Edwards); S, T, harp. MS: A [Welsh text: no. 2]

Nine Welsh Folksongs: I Ffarwel i Langyfelach — II Seven Oxen Songs: Llantwit Major, Brecon, St. Athan, Merthyr, Llangynwyd, Margam, Ogmore — III Mari Lwyd; voice, pf. MS: A (II, 1, 2, 6, 7, 4, 3, pubd as Six Welsh Oxen Songs, Boosey & Co. 1937; III pubd Gwyn Publishing Co. 1938) [Welsh texts: I and III]

Welsh Nursery Tunes for BBC 'Children's Hour'; S, B, cl. perc, 2 pfs. MS: B [Welsh texts]

Set 1: Jim Cro, Gee Geffyl Bach, Cadi Ha, Ble 'Rwyt Ti'n Myned, Lali Lwli, Pwsi Meri Mew, Ple'r Ei Di Heno, Modryb Elin Ennog

Set 2: Pry Bach yn Mynd, Deryn y Bwn, Migildi Magildi, Ble'r Ei Di, Oes Gafr Eto?, Robin Ddiog, Mae gen i Gwpwrdd, Si, so Jac-y-Do

Your harps and cymbals (melody by Handel); SSAA, pf. OUP 1951

Three Yugoslav Folksongs: Mary Maiden, Dalmatian Lullaby, The Pearly Adriatic; unison voices/SA, pf (or fl/vl, pf). OUP 1952 (nos. 1 and 3 also arr. A. W. Benoy for unison voices/SA, recorders, str, pf, with various options. OUP 1966)

APPENDIX II

Ave maris stella	Richard Hickox Singers, conducted by Richard Hickox	Chandos, ABRD 1116
Ballads	BBC Welsh Symphony, Orchestra, conducted by Vernon Handley	BBC Artium, REGL 381; reissued (1996) on Lyrita SRCD.327
Carillons	Anthony Camden (oboe), London Symphony Orchestra, conducted by Sir Charles Groves	HMV, ASD 3006; reissued (1995)on Lyrita SRCD.323
Two Choruses: Harp Song of the Dane Women; Mariners' Song	Richard Hickox Singers, Caryl Thomas (harp) Frank Lloyd and Christopher Larkin (horns), conducted by Richard Hickox	Chandos, ABRD 1116
The Dancers	Eiddwen Harrhy (soprano), Caryl Thomas (harp), Richard Hickox Singers, conducted by Richard Hickox	Chandos, ABRD 1116
Fairest of Stars	Janet Price, (soprano), London Symphony Orchestra, conducted by Sir Charles Groves	HMV, ASD 3006; reissued (1996) on Lyrita SRCD.327
Fantasia on Welsh Nursery Tunes	London Symphony Orchestra, conducted by Sir Charles Groves	HMV, ASD 3006; reissued (1995) on Lyrita SRCD.323
Penillion	Royal Philharmonic Orchestra, conducted by Charles Groves	HMV, ASD 2739; reissued (1980) on Oriel, ORM 1001 and (1995)on Lyrita SRCD.323
Sea Sketches	English Chamber Orchestra, conducted by David Atherton	Decca, SXL 6468; reissued (1995) Lyrita SCRD.323
Six Poems by Gerard Manley Hopkins	Helen Watts (contralto), City of London Sinfonia String Sextet	Chandos, ABRD 1116
Symphony no.2	BBC Welsh Symphony Orchestra, conducted by Vernon Handley	BBC Artium, REGL 381; reissued(1996) on Lyrita SRCD.327
Trumpet Concerto	Howard Snell (trumpet), London Symphony Orchestra, conducted by Sir Charles Groves	HMV, ASD 3006; reissued (1995) on Lyrita SRCD.323

BIBLIOGRAPHY

Anon: 'First Woman to Compose Feature Score', *The Cinema Studio* (supplement to *The Cinema*), i/17 (July, 1948), 5.

Boyd, Malcolm: 'Benjamin Britten and Grace Williams: Chronicle of a Friendship', *Welsh Music*, vi/6 (1980).

Davies, Eiluned: 'A Pianist's Note on Grace Williams's *Sinfonia Concertante*', *Welsh Music*, v/9 (1978), 22–9.

Davies, Eiluned: 'Grace Williams and the Piano', *Welsh Music*, vi/4 (1980), 18–25.

Hughes, Arwel: 'Rhai Argraffiadau am Grace Williams', *Welsh Music*, v/6 (1977), 31–2.

Mitchell, Donald and Reed, Philip, ed.: *Letters from a Life: Selected Letters and Diaries of Benjamin Britten* (London, 1991).

Parry, Enid: 'Atgofion am Grace Williams', *Welsh Music*, v/6 (1977), 7–14.

Rees, A. J. Heward: 'Views and Revisions', *Welsh Music*, v/4 (1976–7), 7–18.

Rees, A. J. Heward, ed.: 'Grace Williams: a Self Portrait' *Welsh Music*, viii/5 (1987), 7–16.

Rhys, Dulais: 'Grace Williams trwy Lygaid Myfyriwr', *Welsh Music*, v/6 (1977), 33–4.

Thomas, A. F. Leighton: 'Grace Williams', *Musical Times*, xcvii (1956), 240–43.

Thomas, A. F. Leighton: 'The Music of Grace Williams', *Anglo-Welsh Review*, xv (1965), 90–103.

Various authors: 'Grace Williams: a Symposium', *Welsh Music*, v/6 (1977), 15–30; v/7 (1977–8), 41–60.

Warkov, Esther R. 'Traditional Features in Grace Williams's "Penillion"', *Welsh Music*, vii/1 (1982), 15–24.

Whittall, Arnold: 'Grace Williams 1906–1977', *Soundings*, no.7 (1978), 19–37.